IDEOLOGICAL
CONTROL IN
NONIDEOLOGICAL
ORGANIZATIONS

IDEOLOGICAL CONTROL IN NONIDEOLOGICAL ORGANIZATIONS

Barbara Czarniawska-Joerges

PRAEGER

New York
Westport, Connecticut
London

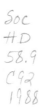
Library of Congress Cataloging-in-Publication Data

Czarniawska-Joerges, Barbara.
Ideological control in nonideological organizations.

Bibliography: p.
Includes index.
1. Organizational effectiveness.   2. Executives.
3. Control (Psychology)   4. Autonomy (Psychology)
I. Title.
HD58.9.C92 1988   658.4'03   87-32759
ISBN 0-275-92794-6 (alk. paper)

Library of Congress Catalog Card Number: 87-32759
ISBN: 0-275-92794-6

First published in 1988

Praeger Publishers, One Madison Avenue, New York, NY 10010
A division of Greenwood Press, Inc.

Printed in the United States of America

The paper used in this book complies with the
Permanent Paper Standard issued by the National
Information Standards Organization (Z39.48-1984).

10 9 8 7 6 5 4 3 2 1

Contents

Figures

Preface

Nowadays it is becoming clear that ideologies, myths, rituals, and the like are full-fledged facets of everyday organizational life. However, such phenomena are usually dealt with at a popular or an ethnographic level of analysis, or, when more seriously treated, still within the disciplines that traditionally dealt with such problems, political science or anthropology. Their significance and their fit into a broader pattern of organizational performance have not yet been studied more thoroughly and systematically. The present book is an attempt in this direction.

By examining a set of empirical cases of use of ideological control in various organizations, I try to arrive at a tentative theory. Each case contributes new grounds for subsequent generalizing and therefore provides a more complete analytical scheme for the next case.

The empirical studies were conducted in three countries and three different economic systems (Poland, the United States, Sweden). However, the studies were by no means comparative in the conventional sense of the word. The different countries were treated as different sites from which to collect the data, with the assumption that each site has a logic of its own. If some comparisons are made, it is only within the specific contexts: no general judgments concerning different systems are produced or attempted.

The empirical basis of this book is derived from the following studies:

- A two-part study on controlling top managers in large organizations in Poland and the United States (1978–1981)
- A project on control processes in declining organizations (1982)
- A study of top managers in a Swedish company (1983)
- A study of general directors in the Swedish public sector (1984)
- A study of Submunicipal committee reform in Swedish municipalities (1985–1986)

With the exception of the last study, all the projects were undertaken within frames of reference other than that of ideological control, and the corresponding parts of the results have been published (see the bibliography). The ideological control aspect emerged slowly, first as an additional issue of interest, then becoming, eventually, the central focus of the final study.

The projects had different sponsors and host institutions, to which I am indebted. They were, in chronological order: Faculty of Management, University of Warsaw; American Council of Learned Societies; Sloan School of Management, M.I.T.; Institute of Comparative Social Research at Science Center Berlin; Swedish Center for the Quality of Working Life; Institute of International Business, Stockholm School of Economics; Swedish Building Research Council; and the Economic Research Institute, Stockholm School of Economics.

The final attempt to analyze the phenomenon of ideological control in organizations was scrutinized and greatly improved by Nils Brunsson, Nina L. Colwill, Bengt Jacobsson, Bernward Joerges, Maj-Britt Johansson Lindfors, Patricia Y. Martin, and Kerstin Sahlin-Andersson. Many thanks to them all.

IDEOLOGICAL CONTROL IN NONIDEOLOGICAL ORGANIZATIONS

1

Organizations, Control, Ideologies

CONTROL VERSUS AUTONOMY

One of the antinomies that for centuries has attracted the interest of students of humanity is the universal need for, simultaneously, freedom and order. Within organizations these two basic human needs take the form of the individual's striving for autonomy and for control. Aristotle, Marx, and generations of organizational theorists and practitioners looked for a viable solution that would permit the preservation of both. Be it a golden mean, a dialectical conflict, or a managing of diversity and independence (Lorsch and Allen 1973), people in organizations try to preserve for themselves both autonomy and control. Both are needed for the survival of organizations and the human beings in them. An extreme position within an organization that neglects the opposing position (that is, with either autonomy or control being strongly dominant) constitutes a serious threat to the organization and its members.

Autonomy for the individual offers organizations flexibility and creativity, which are essential for adaptation to changing environments. Autonomy provides people with opportunities for self-fulfillment and, what is more important, sovereignty, a necessary condition for preserving human dignity and for continuation of life's most important task: the search for meaning. Without autonomy, organizations become rigid and obsolete. Without autonomy, individuals become alienated and apathetic.

Control of others offers organizations predictability, which is necessary to produce standardized outputs and to coordinate actions. Control provides individuals with a tool to cope with the uncertainty and complexity of life. Without control, organization is invaded by chaos and deadly entropy. Without control, individuals are exposed to too much pressure from existential anxiety.

An interesting characteristic of our times is that organizations are able to offer more autonomy to individuals and, at the same time, exert greater control than ever before. The dilemma has not been solved and never will be; the amount of both information and ambiguity increases continuously, creating overload on both organizations and individuals.

Organizational control processes are a fascinating topic that have attracted a great many students. Extensive reviews of the literature are available (for example, Cartwright 1965; Donnelly et al. 1978; Dunbar 1981; Etzioni 1965; Gustafsson 1979), and there is little need to create one more. Nor do I intend to critically evaluate existing theories. (All theories that help to broaden or deepen the understanding of a phenomenon are valid, and will continue to be valid, until another theory offers a better explanation.) My personal interest lies in dealing with aspects of organizational control processes that have not been tackled before.

Organizational control used to be described in disciplinary terms. The dominant point of view might be psychological as opposed to cybernetic, technological as opposed to economic, political as opposed to administrative, but integrative attempts are infrequent. I do not propose to combine all the disciplines in one endeavor. Rather, in my research, I intend to start with the study of organizational control processes as they appear in organizational reality, and let the theoretical explanations be selected by the empirical findings. Thus the interpretation of data may require excursions in some or all of the fields I have mentioned. This is a more feasible undertaking than trying to coordinate them a priori in a theoretical framework that encompasses all possible disciplines. Such an inductive, interdisciplinary approach is relatively new in the social sciences, which means that there are no ready models to follow. Research sometimes becomes a painful learning process where mistakes count more than achievements. It is nevertheless very rewarding, and therefore worth continuing. It requires openness at the beginning of the research process, a continuous search for methods and techniques, and a selective approach to literature.

Organizational control, even if studied on the level of middle-range collectives (where social structures can be proved to exist, in contrast with macrocollectives, such as social classes, which are basically rhetorical classifications, or micro, psychological descriptions of individuals, where they are neglected; Harré 1978), is understood and studied as managerial control over nonmanagerial organizational levels. That focus of interest persists in spite of the fact that the dilemma of joining autonomy and control is much greater on higher levels. Yet this problem receives little attention. As Etzioni puts it, "Much more is known about control over lower-ranking participants than of higher-ranking ones, and clearly, the control of the higher ranks is at least as important" (1965, p. 674).

There are several reasons why such control is important. One is that the control of the higher ranks may be crucially important for the relationships of an organization with other organizations and institutions. These relationships are mostly formed by the higher ranks. Another reason for studying control at higher organizational levels is that in our predominantly hierarchical society, the processes taking place at higher levels are always reflected at lower levels. It has always fascinated me, for instance, that union-oriented researchers, preoccupied with control addressed to the shop-floor level, have never paid much attention to what was happening on higher levels. Yet common sense suggests that top managers who are strictly controlled by the corporate executive officer will not create an atmosphere of autonomy and encouragement for their subordinates.

Organizational control was assumed to be organization-specific. Business organizations would use some form of economic control; political organizations, ideological control; and asylums could apply total control (Goffman 1961). While it is undoubtedly true that some types of control are perceived as more legitimate for certain organizations than for others, this organization-specific approach to control processes seems more limiting than enlightening. In addition, researchers tend to specialize according to the type of organization they study, and not to the problems or phenomena that are of interest to them. Yet comparing control processes across different organizations seems to be a necessary step in the process of understanding organizational control.

This book is an attempt to adopt all the above postulates in an empirically based pursuit of an interesting organizational and societal phenomenon: the use of ideological control in organizations that traditionally are not associated with ideologies: economic, business, and administrative organizations. These we shall call nonideological organizations throughout the book.

Before engaging in such an endeavor, one should be reminded that if the phenomenon of ideological control entering all organizations is relatively recent, the topic of ideologies in organizations is certainly not new (see, for instance, Bendix 1970; Perrow 1976; Sjöstrand 1985 for managerial ideologies). In order to be able to analyze empirical cases of ideological control, it is necessary to pass—quickly, I hope— through the jungle of theories and concepts relating to control and ideology in organizational contexts. This exercise should help to establish a vocabulary common to the author and the reader that can be employed in the further analysis.

IDEOLOGY AND ITS ORGANIZATIONAL USES

Dominant Definition

"Ideology" was the name of the new science of ideas, the basis for which was laid in 1797 by Antoine Louis Claude Destutt de Tracy, who wanted it to be new and renewing, positive and empirical, in relation to society (Gouldner 1976). The *idéologues* can be seen as originators of both sociology and positivism. It did not take long, however, before Napoleon called them "impractical, unworthy and unrealistic theorists," setting the tone for centuries to come.

In the ordinary language of everyday life, as in the extraordinary language of sociology (be it academic sociology or Marxist), "ideology" is commonly stigmatized as a pathological object. It is seen as irrational cognition; as defective discourse; as false consciousness; as bad sociology. That low opinion was one reason why some scholars prematurely celebrated "The End of Ideology.'' As the subsequent history . . . demonstrates, the rumors of the death of ideology were much exaggerated. (Gouldner 1976, p. 3)

In critical organization theory, the definition of ideology is that proposed by Marx in his late writings, and developed further by Engels and Althusser. According to it, ideology is a false consciousness (science being the true one; Therborn 1980). Thompson (1980), following Geertz (1964), discusses two social science continuations of this approach: the interest and the strain theories of ideology. A good example of an interest theory definition of ideology in relation to organizations is Bendix's (1970) description of managerial ideologies as ''all ideas which are espoused by or for those who exercise authority in economic enterprises, and which seek to explain and justify that authority'' (p. 529). The strain theory sees the role of ideology in sustaining individuals and groups ''in the face of chronic strain, either by denying it outright or by legitimizing it in terms of higher values'' (Geertz 1964, p. 55). Strains are produced, in modern societies, by the same factors as clashes of interest are. Both theories strive to address the same kinds of problems, in somewhat parallel ways. Both offer value-laden, unifunctional definitions of ideology, neglecting the possibility that ideologies, though heavily value-laden, may still deserve a value-free definition and that they may fulfill many different functions.

Thompson's main objection to both interest and strain theory definitions of ideology is that they seem to suggest the possible existence of unbiased, nonsubjective selectivity—in science. Rejecting this possibility, he joins his predecessors in claiming that ideology is indeed a distorted social construction of reality, and that it serves to support an existing order in organizations.

Ideology functions as an overarching idea-system or symbol-system that provides a protective shield . . . for a version of reality that would minimize the disturbing effects of reinterpretation and reconstruction. It provides a fundamental justification and legitimation for what it would have us believe is an *established order*. It thus provides a rationale for a particular form of selectivity and seeks to exclude others. (Thompson 1980, p. 232)

Interestingly, this definition is, in its most orthodox form, also accepted by apologetic organization theory, as certified by the relative absence of the concept of ideology in most organizational studies. Ideology is something that ought not to be found in business and administrative organizations, which are by definition nonideological. Ideology's place is in political and religious organizations. Everywhere else it is a dangerous aberration and should be eliminated, in order to make room for science. In that aspect the apologists agree with critics: it was Mannheim who first hailed the "death of ideology," destroyed by Marxist science (Mannheim 1936), to be followed by Daniel Bell, who confirmed the "end of ideology" (Bell 1960)—prematurely, as the initial quote from Gouldner indicates. (For an interesting analysis of what he calls "Mannheim's Paradox," an attempt to analyze ideology on nonideological grounds, see Geertz 1964.)

Some more recent studies suggesting the presence of ideologies in nonideological organizations (Meyer 1981; Brunsson 1985) have been perceived as provocative and unconventional when compared to traditional theories. In other studies, the notion of "culture" (Clarke et al. 1979) or "myth" (Jönsson and Lundin 1977; Hedberg and Jönsson 1977) is used as a euphemism for "ideology."

A Broader Definition

The conventional definition of ideology seems to be of limited use in organizational studies. I tend to agree with Therborn (1980), who states that it builds on an untenable image of human motivation:

Human behavior was determined by "interest," by class interests. The forms of consciousness either corresponded to these "interests," as "true" consciousness, or not, in which case they were illusions, and as such ineffective (at least in the longer run). . . .

This notion of motivation by interest assumes that normative conceptions of what is good and bad and conceptions of what is possible and impossible are given in the reality of existence and are accessible only through true knowledge of the latter. (Therborn 1980, pp. 4–5)

This idealistic notion of truth in relation to ideologies is as inappropriate as it was when it was applied to abstract art: the latter was also called a "distortion" of reality. What is more, the general (if very tacit) acceptance of this definition has had, in my opinion, an impoverishing effect on studies of organizations. Critical theories were bound by the narrowness of the concept and its static character (after having stated that capitalist ideology corresponded to false consciousness, one could do little but collect illustrations). Apologetic theorists, on the other hand, were too frightened of the concept to explore its possible organizational referents. Even in recent organizational culture studies, "ideology" is diluted into "ideas," "beliefs," "visions," "images."

Still following Therborn, I would propose to turn attention to an early Marxian definition of ideology, according to which it is a medium through which people make history as conscious actors; be it in an organizational or in a national context. It is not the only means, but probably one of the most important. In that sense, ideologies should be seen in the first place as important vehicles for change and not, as in conventional definitions, as the barriers to change. The October Revolution in the Soviet Union and the Cultural Revolution in China are obvious examples of this thesis. Gouldner (1976), in his somewhat narrower definition (ideologies are symbol systems used to justify and to mobilize public projects of social reconstruction), emphasizes the same change aspect of ideologies. Sjöstrand (1985, 1986) similarly calls for a different definition of ideology in relation to economic organizations.

Therborn describes also the ways in which ideologies influence people:

Ideologies subject and qualify subjects by telling them, relating them to, and making them recognize:

1. *what exists*, and its corollary, what does not exist, what nature, society, men and women are like. In this way we acquire a sense of identity, becoming conscious of what is real and true; the visibility of the world is thereby structured by the distribution of spotlights, shadows and darkness.

2. *what is good*, right, just, beautiful, attractive, enjoyable, and its opposites. In this way our desires become structured and norm-alized.

3. *what is possible* and impossible; our sense of the mutability of our being-in-the-world and the consequences of change are hereby patterned, and our hopes, ambitions and fears given shape. (Therborn 1980, p. 18)

We can say, then, that an organizational ideology is a set (system) of ideas describing the organization-relevant reality, projecting a desired state of affairs, and indicating possible ways of reaching the desired state. When a desired state corresponds to the description of reality, ideology can be seen as eulogistic; when there are no feasible means of change indicated (short of joining the other world), it can be seen as apologetic. But ideologies do not have to be eulogistic or apologetic: they may equally well be critical and constructive.

Such a concept of ideology can easily be used alongside the idea of culture and can clarify the relationship between ideology and science. Accordingly, not all ideologies are or can be used as science (or art or law), but all science is accumulated within specific ideological contexts and therefore can be used as ideology. New discoveries and new theories usually function as liberating devices in relation to old ideologies and as legitimating devices for new ideologies.

However, the constitution of particular discourse called science means neither that its practice is or will remain immune from the subjectivity of its practitioners, nor that it is incapable of affecting the subjectivity of the members of society, of functioning as ideology. (Therborn 1980, pp. 2–3)

Analogous reasoning can be applied to the reverse process: ideological impact upon science via the subjectivity of researchers. It would be naive or hypocritical to believe that such an influence can be eliminated. What can and should be attempted, however, is a deepened and probing self-reflection on the part of researchers, so as to account for as many ideological influences as one can detect in oneself. The alternative is, of course, the conscious use of science in the service of an ideology. Such an endeavor may be considered unscientific, but it is certainly feasible and, in my opinion, justifiable as long as it is done in the open.

Still more clarity can be achieved by contrasting ideology with other symbolic systems and elements. On the one hand, ideology, through its systemic, reality-explaining character, approaches world view and value system. One could say that ideology is a world view enriched by a vision and a prescription for action. Value systems are more static, less concrete, and less visible than ideologies. Ideologies are presented openly and propagated; value systems can be inferred from ideologies, or revealed in an emergency or as a response to a challenge. In a dynamic perspective, ideologies can be seen as the result of a discrepancy between a world view and a value system.

On the other hand, ideas or norms lack the systemic character: they can be separate and disconnected. Additionally, they do not deal so much with a description of reality as with a desired state: an idea of a product that will sell, a norm describing what is decent behavior toward a competitor.

It is easy to see that there will be many borderline cases where it is hard to decide whether a given product of the human mind is an idea, an ideology, or a world view (how to classify a business strategy?). But unless the purpose of analysis is an exercise in classification, that should not be a serious worry. Fuzzy-edged concepts are of more use in tackling organizational realities, in themselves very fuzzy. Let us, then, accept this imperfect concept of ideology and see how it can be related to control processes in organizations.

FOUR MODES OF ORGANIZATIONAL CONTROL

Organizational control is exercised through a variety of methods, mechanisms, and means, and there have been many attempts to classify them (Dahl 1957; Etzioni 1961; Edwards 1979; Hicks and Gullett 1975; Salaman 1979). The classification criteria are usually forms or means of control (such as coercive control, charismatic control, bureaucratic control) but rarely its target. If I tend to agree with Dahl (1957) that the ultimate purpose of every control attempt is to effect or prevent a change in behavior, I must acknowledge that this purpose is not always reached by direct influence on behavior. A target of control can be a person or the life of a person (persona or total control), behavior (action control), world view (ideological control), or the immediate environment of a person or a group (ecological control) (Czarniawska and Hedberg 1985; Czarniawska-Joerges 1987).

One should expect a relationship between means and targets: certain targets can be reached only if appropriate means are available (for example, ecological control via bribing requires adequate resources), and some means are suited only for certain targets (for instance, persuasion as a means for ideological control). The target-based classification proved to have great value as a systematizing device, and we shall apply it throughout the book.

Total (persona) control aims at affecting the physical and/or mental integrity of individuals. The most typical form it takes is coercion, control that is based on force and consists in use (or the threat of use) of sanctions (Etzioni 1961). As Zimbardo's experiment demonstrated, total control need not have a conscious choice of a target. The experiment consisted in a simulation of a jail (university students played roles of prisoners and wardens, with Zimbardo himself as the chief warden) and was never completed according to the original design: the simulation became too real. The "wardens" were expected to exercise some form of action (behavioral) control, but they moved toward total control and started to humiliate and mistreat the "prisoners" (Zimbardo et al. 1974).

It may seem that total control is limited to totalitarian institutions or that it ended together with the primitive stages of early industrialization. However, layoffs may be seen as illustrations of the same mode of control, as shown by cases of suicide and heart attacks. The control is then aimed toward both those who leave and those who stay.

Action (behavioral) control is the mode most often discussed in relation to nonideological organizations like business and bureaucracies. Supervision, technological control, and bureaucratic control (Edwards 1979) can all be seen as different forms of action control, and so can the piece-rate system. Direct supervision, rules, regulations, and performance-specific incentives are all means of direct influence where behavior is the target. In contemporary organizations, this mode of control is the most typical, as it stems from a work contract giving one party a right to influence another party's behavior.

Ideological control targets the organizational members' perception of reality by offering attractive goals and convincing interpretations. Ideologies are both targets and means of control: new ideologies are supposed to replace the old ones, organizational ideologies should take the place of individual ones, and so on. Adhering to a "right" ideology is a source of many social and psychological rewards: social acceptance, a sense of belonging, reduced uncertainty. Deviation produces corresponding punishment: a feeling of isolation, cognitive dissonance, possible open criticism.

Ecological control is a structuring of individuals' or groups' immediate environment so that certain actions (desired by a controller) become preferable to others. This mode of control has attracted the least attention of organization researchers, possibly for two reasons. One is that the use of ecological control indicates that the potential subject of control is not directly accessible to a potential controller. Persons, actions, and ideologies are not within the reach of the source of control, and only the environment can be affected, in the hope that it will bring about a desired change in behavior. Bribes are, as mentioned before, good illustrations of means used for ecological control. The person who offers a bribe can only hope that it will prove effective, as persons who get the bribe still have full freedom to do as they please.

Input control (Scott 1981) is another example. It is often used by politicians against administrators when they feel that rules will not produce desired actions (if, for example, innovative behavior is needed) or that their ideology does not have the same impact backstage as it does on stage, or when they are more interested in showing their intentions than in actual control (Czarniawska-Joerges 1986).

All modes of control are usually present, in different degrees, in all organizations. Still, one can speak of a dominant control mode, the mode that is most visible at a given time in a given organization. Also, all modes can have an oppressive or a benevolent form. Total control in the case of severely handicapped individuals is generally approved of in Western societies. Action control can be a Kafkaesque trap of the blind bureaucracy or a source of useful feedback on performance. Ideological control can oscillate between brainwashing and enlightenment. Ecological control can be realized by creating attractive working environments, as in Silicon Valley, or by structuring the whole ecology of people, reducing them to puppets with the illusion of freedom, as in *Walden Two* (Skinner 1970). Of course, the judgment is mine: Skinner saw his utopia in entirely positive terms:

Now, that we *know* how positive reinforcement works and why negative doesn't, . . . we can be more deliberate, and hence more successful, in our cultural design. We can achieve a sort of control under which the controlled, though they are following a code much more scrupulously than was ever the case under the old system, nevertheless feel free. They are doing what they want to do, not what they are forced to do. That's the source of the tremendous power of positive reinforcement—there's no restraint and no revolt. By a careful cultural design, we control not the final behavior, but the *inclination* to behave—the motives, the desires, the wishes. (Skinner 1970, p. 262)

I am quoting Skinner at some length to focus on an interesting aspect of his utopia: he hoped to achieve action control via ideology produced by ecological control! The most immediate target is the ecology of the inhabitants of Walden Two: they live in an environment of carefully constructed positive reinforcements. Such a situation should automatically produce an ideology in which behaviors desired by the creator of the environment are the same as those desired by people themselves. The ideal of all the controllers seems to be the same: to make people do what they should be doing on the basis of their own wishes.

Previous Descriptions of Ideological Control

Traditional approaches limited the occurrence of ideological control to ideological organizations—that is, political and religious ones, with the possible extension to educational organizations. Outside these, ideological control was seen as "unnatural" and even dangerous because of specific definition of ideology.

Since Weber's time much has been said about the role of charisma in organizational control, but charisma is not the same as ideological control. An effective ideology does not require the presence of a charismatic leader (they are quite scarce, anyway), and it involves more complicated social mechanisms than identification and modeling. In fact, ideological control occurs in organizational life much more often than organization theory would predict.

To claim that attention to ideology's controlling function in nonideological organizations is only recent would be inaccurate. The controlling use of ideology was observed, under different names, in a variety of organizations. Most of those observations focused on moral extremes: ideological control as the epitome of organizational evil or as an ideal to strive for.

Convincing examples of the former can be found in a literary form: Huxley's *Brave New World* and Orwell's *1984* are striking illustrations of misuses of ideological control. If we leave fiction, Schein's (1961) extraordinary report of the brainwashing performed on U.S. POWs imprisoned in China during the Korean War would be an example, even if approaching the realm of total control. And, finally, closer to home, our everyday organizations:

> . . . is it not the supreme and most insidious exercise of power to prevent people, to whatever degree, from having grievances by shaping their perceptions, cognitions and preferences in such a way that they accept their role in the existing order of things, either because they can see or imagine no alternative to it, or because they see it as divinely ordained and beneficial? (Lukes 1974, p. 24)

The other extreme emphasizes only the positive aspects of ideological control. Even if March and Olsen, in their review of administrative reforms in the last century in the United States (1983), do not use the term "ideological control," they are very aware of it. In their conclusion concerning the strange fate of reforms ("few efficiencies are achieved; little gain in responsiveness is recorded; control seems as elusive after the efforts as before," p. 288), the reforms are seen as a form of public education. This observation leads them to a reformulation of the definition of governance as a creation of meaning: ". . . governance is an interpretation of life and an affirmation of legitimate values and institutions" (March and Olsen 1983, p. 293).

The history of organizational theory (and some other social sciences) resembles a journey through innumerable Scyllas and Charybdises, where salvation always comes as an apprehension of the fact that everyday reality seldom contains extremes, and is full of shades of gray. Ideological control may be beneficial and may be damaging, and very often is both, at different times and for different groups. Therefore, instead of delivering an a priori moral judgment on it, let us focus on its character. The endeavor is helped by the fact that research fashion has just turned this way.

Sign of the Times or a Fad in Organization Theory?

Imagine a scriptwriter who plans an updated version of *Quo Vadis*. The script might develop along the following lines:

The manager of a 100-person sales branch rented the Meadowlands Stadium (New Jersey) for the evening. After work, his salesmen ran onto the stadium's field through the players' tunnel. As each emerged, the electronic score-board beamed his name to the assembled crowd. Executives from corporate headquarters, employees from other offices, and family and friends were present cheering loudly. . . .

Or, the same writer, looking for topics, may take inspiration from the behavioral sciences, as has been done before. After having read about Köhler's (1940) famous experiments with problem-solving monkeys (who received a banana for every aha! insight into the problem), he can transpose the theme to modern times without difficulty:

At . . . a technical advance was desperately needed for survival in the company's early days. Late one evening, a scientist rushed into the president's office with a working prototype. Dumbfounded at the elegance of the solution, and bemused about how to reward it, the president bent forward in his chair, rummaged through most of the drawers in his desk, found something, leaned over the desk to the scientist, and said: "Here!" In his hand was a banana. . . .

Perhaps both situations lend themselves best to some sort of grotesque comedy, with a touch of tragedy. Then the following could fit well into the repertoire of our writer:

At Frito-Lay we hear stories, perhaps apocryphal, probably not—it doesn't matter—about people slogging through sleet, mud, hail, snow, and rain. They are not delivering the mail. They are potato chip salesmen, upholding the "99.5% service level" in which the entire Frito organization takes such pride—and which is the source of its unparalleled success.

Comic? Or strangely familiar? These are not Hollywood scripts, but "lessons from America's best-run companies" (Peters and Waterman 1982, pp. xxiv, 70–71, and xxi, respectively). In 1982 the bookstore shelves held a book written by two leading McKinsey consultants, Thomas J. Peters and Robert H. Waterman, Jr. Forty-three weeks later, *In Search of Excellence* was still heading the best seller list, in the meantime having been translated into a growing number of languages. Peters and Waterman's compendium of lessons from America's best-run companies contained a normative message of great attraction, based both on theories and on common sense, plus illustrations excerpted from organizational reality, that proved breathtaking for some readers.

Such readers, dumbfounded by the absurdity of such stories and bemused at how to react to them, may ask why people are willing to run around stadiums if they are neither early Christians nor sportsmen. Why are they pleased with bananas and reconciled with patronizing? Why should anybody want to deliver potato chips in hail? What does it all mean?

It means that the Americans have learned their lesson from the Japanese. It means that today's organizations are increasingly controlled ideologically. This message was formulated as a warning by Whyte in 1956, but the "organization man" was easily discarded as an externally controlled, reactive, and passive aberration. Today's organization men simply internalize organizational values and need no other control. After all, to deliver potato chips through hail, one has to believe in potato chips. And this is not a belief with which we are born.

Peters and Waterman note that the business press since 1980 has started to use "culture" as a main organization metaphor. The media are usually the first to reflect changing practice. Now it is time for theory to follow. One can speculate on the role of multinational companies as creators of demand for studies concerning relationships between organizations and cultures. Alternatively, one can point out the postulates of writers like Dahl (1961), Geertz (1964), and Olsen (1970), who called for analysis of symbols in society in general and in organizations in particular.

Be that as it may, organization theory tries to follow, as the flood of publications on "organizational culture" shows. The most distinct trait of this literature is that it redefines the role of organizational leaders:

The leader can perhaps best be described as a "surf-rider", whose problem is to keep balance and who has little control over what happens or the direction in which he is going. This thought raises the question of the role of leadership in partially controllable systems. The problem might be how to keep balance and how one best utilizes waves and currents. Leadership might be the ability to choose which waves to follow. . . . The leadership problem might be to control the stream of ideas in the organization, to consciously try to influence the ideology instead of making decisions and taking concrete actions, as traditional management wisdom proposes. (Ohlsson 1978, p. 166)

This idea of a different concept of leadership was further clarified by Smircich and Morgan's definition of leadership as "management of meaning":

Leadership is realized in the process whereby one or more individuals succeed in attempting to frame and define the reality of others. Indeed, leadership situations may be conceived as those in which there exists an *obligation* or a perceived *right* on the part of certain individuals to define the reality of others. (Smircich and Morgan 1982, p. 258)

New phenomenon or new definition? Most likely both. The changing character of the labor force (mainly the increasing education level) may render certain modes of control obsolete or inadequate; new concepts or new definitions make organizational members aware of certain phenomena that might have been taken for granted, and create an opportunity to make active use of them or to actively oppose them.

Among many and pressing responsibilities of leadership, there arises a need to develop a *Weltanschauung*, a general view of the organization's position and role amongst its contemporaries . . . the search for stability and meaning, for security, is unremitting. It is a search which seems to find a natural conclusion in the achievement of a set of morally sustaining ideas. . . . (Selznick 1966, p. 47)

What was, at the time Selznick wrote this, only one among many responsibilities slowly grew into a tentative picture of management as a symbolic process (Pfeffer 1977) to become, eventually, *the* manager's role. Managers, who were supposed to make decisions and devise strategies, are now expected to create cultures and invent ideologies. In that endeavor they are assisted by consultants and organization researchers.

Present Research on Ideological Control

Among works focusing on organizational cultures, there are not many dedicated to ideological control, especially on the empirical level. As discussed in the section "Ideology and Its Organizational Uses," the late Marxist definition of ideology is mostly to blame. Among those few that do concentrate on ideological control in nonideological organizations, three approaches seem to be typical: critical, ethnographic, and critical-ethnographic.

The critical approach tends to employ the "ideology-as-distortion" definition and

. . . a Hegelian and Marxist concept of critique which aims at the broadening of human consciousness, the critique of ideological distortion of reality, and the emancipation and liberation of concrete actors and groups through their involvement in collective self-transformation and praxis. From this perspective, critique aims at revealing the historically embedded, partial, and ideological nature of organizational theories as well as the material interests involved in the struggle over organizational knowledge and the definition of organizational reality. (Heydebrand 1985, p. 1–2)

Works of Alvesson (1985a, 1985b), Benson (1977), Edwards (1979), Clegg and Dunkerley (1980), and Salaman (1979, 1980) belong to this category. Unlike the other two approaches, the empirical research serves here only as an illustration of a theoretical, critical thesis.

There is one more work that should be mentioned in this context, even if it is apologetic rather than critical and does not share the Marxist background of the critical approach. It is John Meyer's "They Also Serve: Organizations as Ideological Systems" (1981), which states that organizational formal structures, far from being useless, serve to legitimate organizational action by incorporating the ruling ideology. In light of this statement, the discrepancy between formal and real structure of an organization should not cause astonishment: the two do not have much in common, as they serve different purposes. From the point of view of this book, however, Meyer describes a case of ideological control directed outside the organization, external ideological control, whereas all cases presented in this book deal with the internal ideological control.

The ethnographic approach, in its most typical form, is rich in "thick description" and poor in theory. The readers gain familiarity with a specific piece of organizational reality, usually a small one, and confirm their suspicion that ideological control does take place in organizations (see, for instance, Abravanel 1982). Positive exceptions allow for more general observations, be it through inductive theory building or through comparisons with other works. Cohen's study of the power elite in Sierra Leone (Cohen 1981), Van Maanen's (1974) study of police work, Kunda's (1984) presentation of the Israeli probation agency, and analysis of the culture of Digital Computers (Kunda 1986) provide interesting examples of the ethnographic approach. However, this approach seems invariably to suffer, from the limitations inherent in the present state of anthropology and ethnography as disciplines. First, with the exception of Cohen's work (1981) and Van Maanen and Barley's (1984) announced intention of studying occupational communities, the studied organization seems to be an island, isolated from any social continent.

Second, as the founders of anthropology hardly spoke native languages, the natives are rarely partners: they can be observed or recorded while speaking, but rarely talked to. The researchers, while embarking on explanatory and analytic vessels, provide us with extremely imaginative speculations that, however, could be cut short by asking the natives for explanations of their behavior. This is not to suggest that organizational members have the only right theory of their behavior or that, even if they do, they will willingly share it with researchers. However, people's interpretations and explanations seem to be as interesting a source of data as their straightforward utterances and observable actions. Reflection and analysis are not capacities naturally restricted to the subspecies of researcher.

Third, the emerging cases, even if they focus on the same organizational processes, do not seem to accumulate into a growing body of a theory. It is not that with each study we know more about ideological control: we collect one more illustration of a theory that must be written by somebody else.

The third approach seeks to overcome these shortcomings. The approach, which I chose to call "critical–ethnographic," corresponds roughly to what Heydebrand (1985) calls "neo-Marxist critical organizational theory," and describes as follows:

1. On the level of description and interpretation, it seeks to understand the internal meanings, actions, and relations of an organization and of individual actors from the *standpoint of the participants*. . . .
2. On the level of naturalism or realism . . . the critical model seeks to explain . . . empirical uniformities and regularities from *the standpoint of the observer*. . . .
3. On a third, meta-theoretical level, critical theory seeks to explain the limits and dynamics of these empirical-realist theories themselves. (Heydebrand 1985, pp. 6–8)

In other words, Heydebrand postulates a theory that combines a subjective (interpretive) approach with an objective (explanatory) approach and a reflexive (self-critical) approach. These postulates turn out to be extremely difficult to fulfill in organizational research. Michael Rosen's work can illustrate this point (Rosen 1985). Beautifully rendered and acute ethnographic reports from organizational life, of an unparalleled originality and depth, are contained in a separate part of his report, after which comes, non sequitur, a theoretical part concerned with critical analysis of the societal order, very much along the lines of the traditional critical approach. Michael Burawoy (1979) made similar efforts, less ethnographically oriented and therefore with a smaller gap between the two levels, and with an attempt to introduce a third, self-critical, level.

One of the main difficulties in a skillful combination of all three postulated levels of analysis seems to be an a priori derogatory attitude, which requires mechanical adaptation in order to survive all three levels. Yet an effective critique should require a more balanced picture, in which the whites are carefully analyzed in order to better understand the blacks. The first, interpretive level can hardly benefit from being preceded by the explanatory level. Critical theorists tend to follow in the footsteps of positivists and neopositivists (who are otherwise strongly criticized) in that they know a priori what they are looking for. Instead, one could take the first, interpretative level as the leading one; then look for explanations as they are needed, all the time checking on the process of acting on both levels and bridging them. This commonsense strategy will direct our analysis of empirical cases of ideological control.

CASES OF IDEOLOGICAL CONTROL

The puzzlement experienced while reading works like Peters and Waterman's made me reanalyze my previous studies on organizational control and take a closer look at organizational reality. The studies collected in this book were not, however, designed with the purpose of analyzing ideological control. It is impossible to study ideological control by design. To study a phenomenon, one must look for objects that are reasonably certain to host it. It is certain that in all organizations control processes are present, but it is impossible to say a priori what character they have. The only way is to study organizational control, and then decide on its character after the study or during it. This means, however, that the traditional choice of study objects is out of question if one does not want to create self-fulfilling prophecies.

The first study reported in this book focused originally on the problems of changing control patterns in a situation of economic decline. The Polish leaders trying to react to the changing economic situation of 1971–81 attempted to steer the economy in various ways: one of them was ideological (Chapter 2).

This first attempt at a specific analysis of ideological control made me aware that the concepts I used are relatively unusual in organizational theory and need clarification: the elements of the cultural context of organizing, such as myths, platitudes, rituals. I tried to achieve this clarification by recurring to earlier empirical studies (conducted in

Poland, the United States, and Sweden) that, though not focusing on ideological control, nevertheless improved my understanding of the role of symbolic elements in organizations (Chapter 3).

Continued research on declining organizations brought further examples of ideological control. My study of a Swedish company led me to a similar study by another author (Berg 1979) that additionally illustrated my case. The motivational contexts of acceptance of ideologies became more clear (Chapter 4).

Finally, growing analytical apparatus allowed me to adopt the perspective of ideological control as a main frame of reference in another empirical study, this time of organizational change. The reform of Swedish local governments gave me an opportunity for a complete study of ideological control (Chapter 5).

The theory of ideological control in nonideological organizations is, however, far from complete. Theory building is an ongoing process, say Glaser and Strauss (1974), whose "grounded theory" approach I used throughout my empirical studies. Chapter 6 reflects my understanding of the mechanism of ideological control as it is at present. I found it mature enough to share with readers, but certainly not final. No doubt there is much more to explore and much more to add. One element is missing by design. My purpose is not to produce a final evaluation of the phenomenon or recommendations concerning it. It is up to the reader to make such judgments, if needed. I was led by curiosity and a wish to understand—and I try to share the results. The shelves of works on organization theory are filled with prescriptions, recommendations, and indictments. I do not feel an urge to contribute one more.

2

Ideological Control in
a Planned Economy

THE POLISH ECONOMY, 1970–74

I came across the first case of ideological control while studying the dynamics of control in declining organizations (Czarniawska and Hedberg 1985; Czarniawska-Joerges 1987). The Polish economy in the years 1971–81 had been chosen as an example of an organization that had undergone a severe economic crisis. Following Granick's (1975) example, I decided to treat the whole of the Polish economy as one organization because of its centralized and planned character. From the point of view of Williamson's (1981) classification, one can speak about a hierarchy-type (as opposed to a market-type) economy, and a common hierarchy makes it into one organization. The unity of political and economic power promotes the first secretary of the Polish United Workers' Party (PUWP) to the chief executive officer of such an organization. The hierarchy is, indeed, structurally organized like that of an enormous corporation.

December 1970 was a memorable month for Poland. The workers in coastal factories went on strike to protest raised food prices; inept negotiations led to the use of violence on both sides. Many workers were killed, a few buildings of PUWP committees were burned. In this precarious situation a new first secretary, Edward Gierek, was brought forward. He condemned the use of violence against workers, admitted the bad shape of the economy (quite inaccurately, as later investigations have shown), and humbly asked for help in building a better future. Maybe not all believed him, but many wanted to. And so the foundation for future ideological control was laid.

The first success of the new first secretary was international: he secured large loans from Western banks in order to restructure the ailing Polish economy. He decided to open the previously almost autarkic economy in both directions: increased imports were to be paid for with increased exports. Coal and previously unexploited technological ideas were to become the keys to Western markets.

However, as later analyses showed (Beksiak 1983; Kuczynski 1981), there was nothing basically wrong with the Polish economy in 1970. The problem was political and concerned autocratic decisions of the central leadership: allocation decisions on the proportion of investments to consumption. The Polish economy was on its way to relative independence (exchange mainly within the Council for Mutual Economic Aid), and that transition required massive investments throughout most branches of the economy. Additionally, the previous chief executive officer highly valued economizing and managed to accumulate solid reserves in gold (Beksiak 1982). Such an economic strategy had to be realized at the cost of consumption, and that was why the workers rebelled in 1970.

The new leader used the reserves for a one-time wage and salary increase, and used the Western loans for a dramatic increase in both investment and consumption. But the proportion of the two was as before, or even worse: the relation of gross investment to consumption, stable in 1969–71 (39.8 zloty of investment per zloty of consumption) started to grow, reaching 56.1 in 1978 (Beksiak 1983). Not only were investments very heavy, but their structure was inappropriate (see Beksiak 1983; Kuczynski 1981; Minc 1982).

Therefore, when the oil crisis hit most European economies in 1973, in Poland it enhanced a development that was already well on its way. The loans were used up (the period 1971–73 was an extreme example of ecological control—all changes were stimulating by pouring in new resources, the computer industry being the best example; Bozyk 1983).

The consumption aspirations had grown enormously, compared with the whole postwar period, and the positive effects were nowhere in sight. It was then, in 1974–76, that ideological control became the dominant mode of control in the Polish economy.

PROPAGANDA OF SUCCESS

The ideology I am about to present already had an ironic name at the time of its use: it was called "propaganda of success."

The propaganda of success contained all three parts every ideology has. First, it described the current situation as a failure, a label that was virtually unknown in socialist economies. It was common enough to accuse previous leadership of incapacity and a deviation from the desired road, but then the journey continued "along previously indicated lines," as the militaristic newspeak usually put it, with a different group of leaders. The lines, as Ignatieff observes, were drawn by the great prophet: "The core of Marxian project was to provide a destination for the tragic spiral of need. Communism is a myth of plenitude at the end of time" (Ignatieff 1984, p. 125).

None of the previous ideologies dared to challenge this myth: the moment of deliverance was simply postponed further and further. The propaganda of success, for the first time, promised the deliverance now. Discreetly avoiding confrontation with prophets and neighbors alike, it tied itself to another, much more powerful myth: that of Western affluence. That is well understood by Ignatieff, who says further:

A hundred years later, the societies whose revolutions were inspired by this vision of liberation from history have become dystopias of our time. "Actually existing socialism" has vanquished natural scarcity, but at the cost of increasing relative or social scarcity through the institution of the party *nomenklatura* and its privileges. Having abolished the antagonism of classes based on differential access to property, they have reproduced a new antagonism of classes based on differential access to state power. They are societies as materialist in their common vocabulary of aspiration as any in the West. Indeed, by a perverse irony, the actually existing abundance of Western capitalist society has become the utopia for many inhabitants of actually existing socialism. (Ignatieff 1984, pp. 127–128)

Imagine the success of a leadership that promises utopia today. And more than promises. In December 1970 I was an assistant researcher at the University, earning 900 zloty per month (the equivalent of 10 US$). Within two months my salary was raised by one-third, to 1,200 zloty.

The new leadership had promised that work would be well compensated, and that it would not be as hard as before. "Our young, well educated people," the first secretary used to say, "Must not work with axes and shovels any more" (Czarniawska 1986). In this way, the new ideology tied itself to yet another myth: that of technological backwardness in comparison with the West. Computers were to take the place of abaci, and the most modern tools were to facilitate manual labor. The sphere of consumption was also addressed: Fiats, Coca-Cola, travel to the West, and vinaigrette salad dressing in every grocery shop.

Additionally, the vision part of the new ideology was enticingly packed in a colorful cellophane of nationalism and patriotism, as opposed to the unsuccessful internationalism of the past. Gierek repeatedly said, "We need to build a second Poland, for us and our children." Kurczewski joins my argument: " . . . by wedding a simplified Marxism oriented outwards with an equally simple patriotic organicism for home use, the leadership . . . finally won a mass-scale success in the sphere of ideology" (Kurczewski 1982, p. 22).

How should the promised economic success be achieved? By concrete injections from outside the economy: loans, imported goods, and technologies—at least in the beginning; by a dramatic change in employees' motivation and morale: the recovered trust in their leaders backed by adequate remuneration should produce involvement, commitment, and enthusiasm in work, followed by excellent results, and, finally, by a drastic change in control and organization methods. This postulate, which I am going to discuss at greater length later, alluded to another myth, which I called "a system myth" (see Chapter 3), and to an inferiority complex grounded in a mythological version of Polish history, supposedly tainted by a fatal tendency to anarchy.

Hence, the "propaganda of success" ideology was effective because of its extremely solid anchoring in popular myths: in mythological versions of Poland's and other countries' histories, and in mythological versions of other countries' present reality.

But was the ideology really successful? July 1976 witnessed another attempt to raise food prices, another wave of strikes, another outburst of violence, and a rapid retreat of the leadership. It was then that "propaganda of success" began to mean "propaganda of nonexistent success," and from a successful ideology it turned into a ridicule, and then into an insult (Figa 1982).

What was increasingly lacking was an anchorage in reality. Day after day the workers could watch the "successful production" on the TV screen, only to return to their factories and discover that production was stopped because of non-delivery of spare parts. Galloping inflation soon devoured the pay raises and the loans were long gone, drowned in investments. The strenuous investment program could not be stopped, partly because of investment involvement, and partly because the leadership still hoped for results.

The original question—Why was the ideology successful?—should be rephrased as Why was "the propaganda of success" successful for such a long time? Had nobody noticed that it did not connect with reality?

Some did, but not the majority. The state's monopoly of the mass media allowed it to present only carefully prepared information. And the official statistics were very positive indeed. The loans did not reach a safe level until 1975 and seemed to provide sound grounds for rapid technological development (Pohorille 1982). The crops were extremely good, partly because of good weather, partly because of privatization, which was part of the program. Social services increased by 35 percent in 1971–72, food consumption doubled, and other consumption tripled compared with 1966–70 (Bozyk 1983). The new, dramatically different statistics arrived only after 1976, when the Committee for Workers' Defense (KOR) was formed and began to publish unofficial statistics in underground publications (Kuczynski 1981).

In 1977, an employee of the Office of the Control of the Press, Publications, and Spectacles defected to Sweden, taking some of his working instructions. KOR obtained access to these documents, and soon the censorship rules were commonly known. It was a shock, even at that time, when disenchantment with the ideology was fully grown. As Figa comments:

Until then, everybody knew that the censorship existed, but its picture was one of the unsystematic interventions of an unpredictable apparatus whose activity was connected to temporary difficulties encountered by the rulers. . . .

The reality revealed a well-oiled machinery organized for the explicit purpose of systematic misinformation, distortion and concealment of vital information from the nation. (Figa 1982, pp. 134–135)

The insult was magnified by the fact that misinformation and distortions could continue unopposed for such a long time. Before 1970, it had been taken for granted that the official information was distorted. The appearance of a dialogue between the leadership and shop-floor employees created a hope that the purposeful distortion was over. Therefore the disappointment was that much more bitter.

But it was not only the official information that created a link to a false reality. All who were interested could see the success with their own eyes: full shops, overcrowded parking lots, computers. Because of the rigid and slow-reacting economic system, consumers were able to enjoy goods that were bought or produced in 1971–73 only two to three years later. The reality anchorage weakened slowly and almost imperceptibly. The awakening, even for the most persistent sleepers, came in June 1976.

THE SYSTEMS THEORY AND THE MANIPULATIVE PRACTICE

Imports and increased productivity are the typical ways of saving ailing economies. The remaining way, a change in control structures and organization principles, may also be common, but the direction it takes varies from case to case.

As Kurczewski (1982) notes, the interest in system analysis was prominent in Poland during that period, and certainly was not incidental. Business administration departments started to appear at the universities, and if social engineering was never openly mentioned, management systems were the talk of the day. The "experts' team report" became a popular expression. As was said afterward, in that system the ancient régime courtesans were replaced by experts, and the contacts between Prof. Pawel Bozyk and the first secretary of the PUWP were as important as the contacts between Madame de Montespan and Louis XIV (Kurczewski 1982).

This was a harsh judgment, issued by the opposition on "experts," but it was not without grounds. "Experts" designed new, more perfect "control management systems," in their free time advising managers on how to approach this perfection. My doctoral dissertation (Czarniawska 1980) concerned the managerial incentive systems, and it contained theoretical analysis summarized by four concrete proposals. When presented to practitioners, all four proposals turned out to be highly interesting, but either unrealistic or counteracted by other elements of the central management system. What I, as well as most of my colleagues, did not take into account was the political reality encompassing the economic system. The analytical metaphor I am using in this chapter—that of a planned economy as a single organization—turned into absurdity when taken literally by the system designers.

The system approach and, connected to it, managerial science were, however, the crucial ingredients for the "propaganda of success," and therefore could not be relinquished. What is more, the "propaganda of success" was so strongly and effectively connected to the "system myth" that even when ideology failed, even when success became an empty word, the ingredients remained. It was only a matter of finding a better system.

What was never noticed at that time, and rarely mentioned afterward, was the manipulative character of most managerial prescriptions. When in May 1981, at the Solidarity session on manipulation, I presented a paper titled "Teaching to Manipulate, and the Example of Managers' Training," most of the audience, deeply impressed by the examples of political manipulation, was quite surprised at my theses. Democracy and scientific management were to go hand in hand, safely separated. The ideology had located the center of change within the managerial system, which was to produce the desired result through skillful use of technical and "human" resources. At a time when the concept of ideological control was still very remote from my theoretical frame of reference, the analysis in my paper quite clearly sketched the proposed use of this form of control within the companies. The ideological controllers at the central level advised the use of ideological control at a local level:

The purpose of all managerial courses is obvious: to increase managerial effectiveness. The only problem is that of definition. Two definitions are often in use: one in an economic and another in a psychological context. The former means achievement of maximal results with minimal costs. The latter means maximization of economic results in a way which maximizes organizational members' needs for self-fulfillment and personal development. No sophisticated analysis is needed in order to notice that the two contradict each other, if, of course, we choose to forget the hope that sooner or later they become magically one and the same in that faraway future when the individual interest becomes one with the societal interest.

The managers ask us: how should we solve this dilemma? When the answer remains normative, we say with a great solemnity, that both aspects are important. But when we teach practical skills, a more concrete answer emerges: one can join these aspects by manipulating people so that they will put all their efforts into realization of organizational goals, believing that this is the only sense of their life. . . . Personal development is, after all, a waste of societal resources put into specialization, and creativity is an extravagant challenge to socialization. (Czarniawska, 1981)

The means of achieving the vision was, then, technocrats' control over the rest, skillfully combining system analysis with the human relations approach. Paradoxically, no other Western theories were ever as popular in the official ideology as were these two.

Why did people who opposed the political manipulation allow—encourage—it at the organizational level? One of the possible answers is that management, not only in Poland, is perceived as legitimate manipulation. As long as it does not cross the vital, or perhaps the most visible, interests of employees, manipulation is not opposed; on the contrary, it is welcome as a relief from orders or crude reinforcements. Management systems were, at least in Poland, an escape from arbitrary masters. Their impersonality and "scientific basis," their economic orientation seemed to promise goods long waited for: objectivity, justice, efficiency, affluence. The ideological "how to do it" was very well designed.

ORWELLIAN NEWSPEAK OR IDEOLOGICAL TALK?

The influence of an ideology, an initial condition for control, takes place to a great extent within verbal communication processes, and to an equally great extent uses language as its medium. It has become a tradition to analyze the propaganda used by socialist regimes (not only "propaganda of success," but in general all ways of propagating various ideologies) in relation to the concept coined by George Orwell in his book *1984*: Newspeak. A Polish linguist, M. Glowinski, devoted much attention to this phenomenon, brilliantly comparing the welcome speeches of Edward Gierek and the pope on the occasion of the latter's visit to Poland (Glowinski 1980, 1981). The Jagiellonian University in Cracow in January 1981 organized a session devoted to the phenomenon of Newspeak in relation to the contemporary Polish language. It is therefore easy to conclude that Newspeak served as a medium for spreading the "success" ideology. However, I would like to consider an opposite thesis: that the initial success of the ideology was due, to a great extent, to skillful use of talk that visibly contrasted with the rules of Newspeak.

There are distinct similarities between Newspeak and Newtalk, the ideological talk, that can be misleading. The differences are more important.

Bednarczuk (1985) summarizes Orwell's and Glowinski's analyses as applied to the Polish version of Newspeak. Here are the main characteristics of Newspeak:

1. *Binary evolution.* All statements are moral judgments, with only extreme values possible. With time, the existing terms develop a stable membership (acquired by repetition) in one of the two groups (the "good" group and the "bad" group). Each term acquires an equivalent in the other group. Real-life events can easily be classified according to their relation to other members of the same group: socialism/capitalism, partisan/bandit, intervention/aggression, legitimacy/bureaucracy, agreements/conspiracies, government/regime. The same facts can acquire an opposite meaning by virtue of their connotation: guerrillas fighting a capitalist government are partisans; guerrillas fighting a socialist government are bandits, for instance.

2. *Ritualism as opposed to pragmatism.* The ritual (expressive) function of speech dominates the communicating (instrumental) function: the adherence to a given linguistic procedure is more important than conveying a message. The best-known satirical example is the "every-occasion-speaker" table, where by combining phrases and expressions from various columns, a speaker can create speeches adequate for the May Day celebration, the opening of a factory, or the funeral of a party comrade, as required.

3. *Magicality.* Words create realities and produce a given atmosphere or attitude. That form of influence is probably one of the oldest and best survives in military rhetoric, which is eagerly adopted by the socialist Newspeak: "We retreated to the previously chosen positions" suggests the carefully planned experiment in a war game, and not, as the case most often was, an economic defeat. The exaggerated visions of "enemies" are to produce anger and hatred.

4. *The power to define.* The power group, influencing language usually via censorship and a monopoly on mass media, usurps the right to define the meaning, often contradictory to common use and even to the uses it has previously defined. Hence, "fighting for peace" is fighting for removal of American missiles in Europe, but *not* for withdrawing troops from Afghanistan or for the pacifist anti-draft movement. As the political realities change, and friends become enemies, the definitions have to be accommodated to these changes.

5. *Idiomaticness.* As Newspeak creates its own linguistic repertoire, with an aim to control and limit communication and not to facilitate it (in which it is different from spontaneous language creation and change), there are more and more terms that cannot be translated into "natural" languages. One reason is Newspeak's power to define—the words change meaning almost daily; another is rituality—the pure form is much more difficult to render in translation than are the contents.

6. *Selectivity.* Newspeak systematically impoverishes the language by cutting out the words, expressions, and meanings that connote the reality not desired by its users and that cannot be readily adopted through the use of the other characteristics. Thus an expression that is a platitude in Western leftist thought, "workers' solidarity," celebrated a triumphant comeback in Poland in 1980, where it had been forbidden since the late 1950s.

Magicality and selectivity are strong similarities between Newspeak and ideological talk. The rest of the characteristics are, however, applicable to both only to a very small degree—to the degree that they denote any attempt at persuasion through language.

This thesis had a very convincing illustration in the analysis of a speech delivered in 1977 by Maciej Szczepanski, then president of the Radio and TV Committee in Poland (Marczak 1979). Szczepanski was one of the main engineers of the "propaganda of success" ideology, and his position made him responsible for the function we are discussing now: talk as a medium for ideology's controlling function. Here are the main aspects of Szczepanski's speech, as contrasted with the typical traits of Newspeak.

Newspeak is, basically, a monologue, the function of which is not so much to convey a message as to produce a noise preventing the formulation and reception of messages. A machinelike inhabitant of the world of *1984* is supposed to automatically fall asleep when the voice of the leader reaches him. As such, Newspeak is peculiarly inadequate for conveying ideologies. For the latter the receiver has to listen, to understand, and to believe the message—and therefore a condition of a true (or at least a simulated) dialogue must be created. Edward Gierek spent the first days after his coming to power in factories, explaining economic problems to workers and asking them, looking straight in their faces: "Shall you help me?" And many said, "We shall." Only when the ideology failed did these "consultations with the people" turn into a ritualistic performance, the more embarrassing because of their previously authentic character.

Next, says Marczak, if Newspeak, because of its rituality, is actually a set of platitudes, ideological talk carefully avoids them: the personal character of dialogue requires warmth, spontaneity, and freshness. Quite naturally, I would add, tropes become a most typical means of expression. "The second Poland," "the moral renewal," "a Pole can do all," and many other tropes were to convey the image of success and the way to it.

Apart from avoiding platitudes and introducing successful metaphors, ideological talk reaches for commonly shared meanings, repeating and strengthening the ideology's anchorage in the culture. Gierek and his collaborators dropped concepts like "working class," "our party," "false awareness," and the like to reintroduce "national feeling of belongingness," "personal interests" (which from now on were to gain from societal interests and not vice versa), and "realism." The latter is of particular interest to Marczak and me, as it illustrates a specific symbolic operation that is typical of all ideologies but especially interesting in this case.

Newspeak creates a certain version of reality, mostly by excluding alternatives: here is where the mechanism of noise production is so useful. Ideological talk, using persuasion, suggests a desired choice among existing alternatives. In the case of the "propaganda of success" the vision of reality offered by the ideology was portrayed as "objective and rational," and the alternatives as "subjective and irrational." The reality, with which the "propaganda of success" encouraged confrontation, was not seen in terms of binary values. It was complicated, difficult, and complex, and no leadership could promise to deal with it. Dealing with reality remained the sole function of an individual, and the only help she or he could get was the objective, rationalist vision completed by those who can see further.

This is not, however, a reality that could be influenced, or shaped—even to a limited degree—but a sui generis absolute, against which we are helpless, as it is not a result of our action and the resistance to it. The state of affairs turns out to be fatalistically stable, "metaphysically" irreversible. Any attempts to change it are seen as irrational dreams of subjectivity, which should be confronted with the Objective Rationality of what exists somehow on a metaphysical guarantee. (Marczak 1979, p. 112; translation by B. C. J.)

The "neutrality" of systems theory and other rationalistic concepts was offered as a language appropriate for reality analysis, one that, by pure logic, leads to the same vision of reality as presented in the ideology. The "propaganda of success" as ideology was, indeed, grounded on extreme paradoxes. Preaching success, it was supposed to be most effective in times of failure. Based on nonrational means of influence, it used rationality as its main language. Calling for openness and dialogue, it used this call to distort information on a scale unknown before. These paradoxes, contributing to most of its success, also became its undoing. The irrational ideology of rewards postponed to the next world, offered by many religions, does not solve the dilemmas of modern life, but by the same token is less vulnerable to them.

In order to compare Newspeak with ideological talk, one can use an analogy of artificial intelligence language compared with that of Gabriele d'Annunzio, an Italian poet and writer (1863–1938) famous for his manneristic language. The main similarity of their function is that they both serve to differentiate between in-group and out-group members. But the out-group in Newspeak and artificial intelligence situation is nonexistent: not using that language expels an individual from the world of Newspeak or artificial intelligence. Adopting Newtalk or joining the d'Annunzio fan club creates certain rewards, and dropping the language produces certain punishments, but the alternative realities do not cease to exist. There are always competing ideologies and competing literary styles. Also, Newspeak and artificial intelligence are very poor languages compared with the "natural" languages. Newtalk and d'Annunzio make full use of natural language and embellish it with new metaphors, colorful labels, and poetic devices.

It is quite clear that Newspeak and ideological talk require different situations and are addressed to different groups. The effective introduction of Newspeak is usually backed by force, and its recipients have no alternatives. The effective use of ideological talk requires a sophisticated reward system: not carrot-and-stick reinforcement of particular language uses, but something more absolute:

More important than any immediate gains is a promise of security, a promotion of a belief dictated by traumatic traditionalism, that risk is worthless, because the world stands still. There is no solution for all, but we can save ourselves as individuals. Woe betide the unruly changers of the world, as only those will be saved who humbly seek protection under the wings of Authority, who is eternal and by all the gods of the motionless history blessed with the sign of "rationalist sacrum". (Marczak 1979, p. 114, translation by B. C. J.)

This is the final paradox of the "propaganda of success": the "change through no change" message. But this also makes it closer to the majority of typical organizational ideologies, which preach change in the name of status quo and, while doing so, use the vocabulary of rationality.

To sum up, Newspeak is a medium appropriate for total control; indeed, the actual cases of it were observed in total regimes: in the socialist countries during the Stalinist era and in Campuchea under Pol Pot. Ideological talk is appropriate for ideological control and, as such, loses its grip when alternative ideologies or representations of reality start to prevail. To illustrate this point, let us look once again at the moment when the "propaganda of success" encountered the economic reality: 1976. The ruling team tried to use another resource within the domain of talk: labeling. The more and more visible economic failure was labeled "crisis," and a panic retreat from the assumptions of the economic reform was labeled "economic maneuver." While the latter is not only a label but also a metaphor coined in this particular situation, "crisis" is a very well-known label and can be discussed in more general terms. To call a set of events a "crisis," says Edelman (1977, p. 44), implies certain beliefs:

1. This event is different from the ideological and social issues we routinely confront, different from other crises, and it occurs rarely.

2. It came about for reasons outside the control of political and industrial leaders, who are coping with it as best as they can.

3. The crisis requires sacrifices in order to surmount it. . . .

As I stressed earlier, the effectiveness of the "propaganda of success" lay in its originality, in its successful linkage to accepted elements of culture. The "crisis" label produced the most undesirable linkage of the same sort. The Polish postwar economy was nothing but a chain of "crises," always unique and always rare, never caused by the leaders and ever paid for by the sacrifices of the rest. The participants in the economic life saw the empty shelves in the stores and the word "crisis" in the newspapers. "Oh, no, not this again" was the reaction that finished the era of ideological control. "Magicality" was worn out: words could not produce realities any longer.

SUMMARY

The case of "propaganda of success" informs us of basic conditions facilitating the effective use of ideology in its controlling function. An ideology must be skillfully related to commonly accepted elements of a broader cultural context, which we call "cultural anchorage." Further, an ideology, as a symbolic entity, cannot be confirmed or verified by reality. Ideology is an interpretation of reality, and therefore confirmation can only be a repetition of the same interpretation. An ideology, however, can be challenged by a powerful different interpretation of reality (not necessarily ideological, that is, even without a vision and a formula to achieve it). This is called a lack of "reality anchorage." Cultural anchorage is an accepted connection between the ideology and a cultural context. Reality anchorage is an interpretation of reality that, however loosely, connects the vision part of the ideology to observable reality. In the case discussed, we encountered a negative version of the concept—the lack of reality anchorage, which challenged the ruling ideology.

We shall return to both kinds of anchorage in the cases that follow. However, the present discussion brought to light various other symbolic and cultural elements to which ideology may be related. Therefore, it should be fruitful to establish the place of ideology among other symbolic acts in organizational contexts before we move any further. This will be done both with some additional empirical material, standing beyond the issue of ideological control, and with some conceptual and theoretical classifications. Thus equipped, we can return to a more detailed examination of concrete examples of ideological control in organizations.

3

Ideologies and Other Symbolic Elements

MYTHS OF ORGANIZATIONAL EFFECTIVENESS

In 1978–80, I studied control relationships between the central head-quarters and the companies in Polish "centrals of trade," which were organized along the same lines as large retail corporations in Western countries. The study was extended to U.S. retail corporations in 1981–82 (Czarniawska 1985a). Finally, in Sweden I studied the same kind of relationships between the general directors of central public agencies and their ministries (Czarniawska 1985c).

I asked the managing and general directors questions concerning their mutual expectations, how they are transmitted, what incentives or sanctions are connected with their fulfillment. I never asked my respondents what makes management processes effective, nor did I try to discover their evaluation of the system within which they were operating. Nevertheless, they spontaneously discussed these matters. Their opinions revealed some interesting patterns, which I called the myths of origin of organizational effectiveness (Czarniawska 1986). Before I present them, though, some explanation is required concerning myths as such.

In everyday language, a myth is an erroneous belief that is adhered to against any evidence. As Cohen (1969) puts it, "My beliefs are a strong conviction, yours a dogma, his a myth." However, this is not the original or scientific meaning of the term. Myth, unlike an idea or an ideology, is a narrative of events. Unlike history, however, this narrative has a sacred character, and the notions of truth and falsehood have no relevance for it. The narrative refers in a dramatic form to origins or transformations, which makes myth more important than a simple story, a legend, or a folktale. Hence, there are myths explaining origins of life and myths explaining the origins of the universe, and also myths explaining the origins of organizational effectiveness. Myth offers a socially shared explanation of important phenomena (Cohen 1969).

What is the role of myths? In the first place, they serve as explanations of origins or transformations (and, of course, as a way of blocking alternative explanations). They anchor the present in the past and therefore help to preserve continuity and stability, which are important in every social group. They maintain and express social solidarity by expressing social values and reflecting certain (carefully selected) features of social structure. And, last but not least, they resolve oppositions and contradictions, abundant in the actual rules governing everyday life.

This short presentation of the multiple functions of myths makes it clear that myths are very powerful, and very resistant to change. However, they are not immortal. Science cannot kill a myth, even if it can damage it, as happened with the myths of the origin of mankind. A myth dies when it is no longer able to fulfill all the functions listed above. When the social tissue breaks, when reality is too dramatically different from people's wishes and expectations, that is the time for prophecies, which are myths concerning the future. The winning prophecy becomes the next new myth, and the prophet often becomes a hero.

The discovery of the myths of organizational effectiveness made me speculate about their specific use in everyday organizational life. It is interesting to look for their origins and their roots in a national culture, and also to see how they can become a base for organizational control of a kind that escapes a simple, rational explanation (as presented in organizational books on design).

Let us discuss particular myths and their relation to organizational practice. Each presentation starts with a short myth description, reconstructed by me from various elements provided by my respondents.

Myth I: People

A long, long time ago there was a big land where nobody lived. And then, one day, a big ship arrived, carrying the finest, bravest men from the Old Country. Those men and their finest, bravest women set out to conquer the land and to make a New Country out of it, much better than the Old Country ever was. They were alone and had to count only on themselves while fighting against the powerful nature and the frightening savages. But because they were fine, and brave, and determined, they succeeded.

But it was not a paradise, and there were many evils to fight against all along. Still, the brave, fine, and determined always found their way. There was a poor boy who almost starved to death, but one day he got an idea. He bought a jar of pickled cucumbers very cheap, packed them neatly in plastic bags, and started selling them on a street corner very expensively. Soon he was able to start his own business, and within a short time he became the leader of the biggest organizations in the New Country. So what every men and woman should not forget is that behind all big organizations there are people who knew how to be brave and who had ideas.

U.S. respondents, especially at the corporate headquarters level, repeatedly stressed the key role of people in organizational effectiveness. Management became a personal management: the secret of success was very simple, and was limited to proper recruitment, proper incentives, and a work environment enhancing creativity. The myth was retold in many variations. Sometimes the narrators were heroes themselves: it was they who started the business from scratch, and moved from a poor country store to big retail corporations by their will and determination.

As far as the organizational reality is concerned, Chandler's study (1977) of the managerial revolution left no doubt that one of the most important changes was from "personal management" to "systematic impersonal techniques of modern top management" (p. 381). Some respondents from lower levels (below general managers) spoke about this reality. One general manager who had recently been promoted said about his previous job: "In terms of how I implement the job under the existing rules . . . I had my personal autonomy, because my boss knew we had all these systems that literally, if I fell over with a heart attack, would continue to work. . . . "

But maybe this situation is changing. Maybe people do become the most important determinant of large organizations' effectiveness. Can a myth come true? O'Toole (1979), speaking about changing managerial culture, prophesied that economic efficiency would soon be replaced by liberty, equality of opportunity, environmental quality, and full employment. Profit maximization would win over the tendency toward unlimited growth. Loyalty to the system would be sacrificed for intimacy and friendship. People would dominate systems. However, the present political and economic situation makes one skeptical about the imminence of such changes. Rather, if myths help people to cope with the defects of organizational reality, the growing prominence of the "myth of people" (see Peters and Waterman 1982 for a good example) might suggest the opposite developments in reality. As Martin et al. (1983) note, the most common organizational stories deal with discomfort caused by conflict between organizational demands and human needs. The more people lose against systems, the more they need the "people myth," of which the prophecy of the "forthcoming humanism in business" may be well a part.

Myth II: Systems

Far, far away, beyond the oceans, there is a big, powerful country where everybody is happy, free, and rich. Everybody in the country has a big car, a house, and a swimming pool. Some people, who are smarter than others, have several big cars, several houses, and maybe even several swimming pools. That is because the organizations in the country are the best in the world. They can produce anything you can think of—from a spaceship to electronic gadgets you can play with—and they also pay very high salaries to all the people who faithfully work for them.

And this is because the organizations have the best systems in the world. Nobody ever cheats, nobody is allowed to be lazy and do nothing, nobody can create disorder: Systems would not permit it. The wise and fair systems tell organizations what to produce and how to produce it. They say how the people should be rewarded and how they should be punished, how to find the way to the moon and how to fight enemies. The systems are getting better and better, and so the people are getting happier and richer all the time.

The Polish managers and corporate officers formulated as a necessary and sufficient condition for organizational effectiveness the existence and functions of a proper system of management. Such a system must be designed on the basis of scientific principles, must be objective and fair (and therefore impersonal), and must be highly quantified, in order to secure a proper evaluation and feedback. When looking for such systems, the Polish managers and officers would invariably turn to the United States as the country whose economy is the best example of triumphant systems.

As to the Polish reality, perceptions differed according to level. The higher level (the headquarters) insisted that such a system existed, but unfortunately it was being ruined by the erratic behavior of people (from lower levels) who were not suited, or at best not willing, to submit to the organizational imperative. The lower level (managing directors of enterprises) fully agreed with the normative part of the above image, but either believed the system had yet to be designed or suggested that it was the higher level, with its greed for power and personal advantages, that was ruining it. However, all respondents quite consistently presented a picture of reality in which the functioning of organizations depended on individuals, even if such a conclusion was never formulated.

The "system before people" principle is perceived in the West as a trademark of socialist reality. Indeed, the ideology of collectivism assumes that impersonal, quantitative systems are the best way to promote effectiveness and to counteract destructive individualism. If we remain at this level of explanation, we do no more than confirm a trivial stereotype: capitalism favors people, socialism favors systems. What is interesting, though, is the fact that the origins of the "system" myth can be traced back to the idealized perception of U.S. reality. Within this idealized perception, the socialist economists and managers repeat the operation in which neoclassical economists excel: they compare an empirical reality of "socialism on earth" with an ideal conception of capitalism (Burawoy and Lukacs 1985). By now it should be clear that, especially in the period under discussion (1970–80) but also earlier and later, the neoclassical economists were much more popular in Poland than any Western Marxists could ever be. And so the basis for an ideology in a socialist economy is the mythological version of a capitalist economy.

But there are many other myths to which various official ideologies alluded with no success. Why was this myth so persistent, both in the official speeches and in private thinking? The complementary myth is that of a "Polish fatal tendency to anarchy," which results from a mythologized version of a long history filled with heroic uprisings but no economic successes. Kurczewski wonders about the inconsistency of this version:

. . . a funny conglomerate of opinions, which can be found when we more or less systematically study the historical consciousness of the Poles, a conglomerate which a historian must view with surprise. In that common consciousness . . . the Home Army and the People's Army (in fact political opponents) fought shoulder to shoulder against the Nazis during the occupation of Poland; Dzierzynski [a famous Bolshevik of Polish origin] and Pilsudzki [a nationalist, anti-Communist leader] were the greatest Polish politicians in the 20th century; and Father Skarga (a celebrated Jesuit preacher, 1536–1612) was the first to criticize the fatal Polish inclinations to anarchy and mismanagement, which criticism was later taken up by the PUWP Central Committee. (Kurczewski 1982, pp. 22–23)

A historian may be surprised, but a student of myths should not. Myths very often allude to history, but they are much more than a simple evocation of historical facts. What is more, history could not serve the same anchoring function for an ideology. If we recall once more the definition of myth (a narrative of sacred quality, which in a symbolic way explains origins or transformations), it should be easy to note the similarities and differences between myths and history. Both are narratives, and both try to explain origins or transformations. A myth is, however, usually narrated in a symbolic form, whereas history is described in a factual way. What is most important is the fact that history lacks sacred character and therefore is open to verification and falsification. To say that democracy is not the greatest European tradition is a sacrilege, whereas to prove that there have been many non-European democracies or that many European "democracies" were actually disguised totalitarian regimes serves to extend our historical knowledge. Historians sometimes engage in combat with myths, with few results: history and myths do not live in the same world. Quite recently the British government sent a formal protest to the Belgian government: the tourist industry in the town of Waterloo has for many years been based on the assumption that Napoleon won the battle.

The above observations apply in full to the next myth, of Swedish origin.

Myth III: Independence

Once upon a time there was a big country, but not many people lived there, as it was very cold. They had their leaders, lawgivers, and tax collectors, but because they lived in such isolation from each other, it was hard to communicate, and some things that were forbidden in one part of the country were allowed in another, and so on. And this was not good, especially when the country had to stand together in an emergency. But then a king came who was very enlightened and had a very clever consultant. The king called all the important people and said:

This is no good. We have to have a central administration so that the laws are equal and the taxes are the same all over. Yet, as I am an enlightened king, I know very well that a centralized administration can be too influenced by my rule. We have had enough of absolute rulers. Therefore the heads of central administration shall be independent, and report their activities only to the Parliament, which represents the wishes of the people (or at least some people). The court intrigues shall not influence the state administration, as happens in other countries that have neither such enlightened kings nor such clever consultants.

The Swedish general directors took great care to explain to me the specificity of the Swedish public sector. This specificity is to be seen in the formal independence of the agencies, which, in contrast with other Western countries, are not the subordinate units within a ministry but constitutionally secured separate bodies. This state of affairs is due to the sacred tradition, as represented in the above myth. As was the case with the confused perception of Polish history, knowledge of Swedish history was not the main point. The respondents did not know which king it was and of what, exactly, his reform consisted. More important was the myth in its symbolic form, giving increased legitimacy to any solutions that related to the myth.

Indeed, the study showed that the mechanisms of control exerted by ministries over agencies are based on a shared ''myth of agencies' independence.'' The historically anchored myth of independence of lower top levels from higher top levels in the Swedish public sector allowed the creation, within the same legal framework, of a range of relations varying from strong independence to close control. Some ministers fully controlled general directors of corresponding central agencies, some had very limited contacts with them, and some general directors fully controlled their ministers.

This coexistence of the myth of independence and varying realities solved the problem of centralized control addressed to so many differing organizational units. Such variety and complexity do not exist in private corporations, which usually settle for a much smaller range of control options. The combination of myth and reality existing in the Swedish public sector allowed for enormous flexibility without challenging the basis of legitimacy. The origin of this balance and, indeed, of the myth itself was firmly grounded in history. The perception of history was in itself an indicator of the prolonged functioning of the myth. Sweden is presented to a foreigner as a country "where decentralization was always the rule in the public sector" or "where strong centralization was always successfully combined with the independence of local units." The latter alternative is further elaborated into a normative picture of "decentralized political control" and "centralized administrative implementation."

And so we come back to where we started: to a myth. By now, however, a more complicated set of relations emerges. Myths are related to other stable and shared elements of a culture, such as societal values, history, and other myths. The sources of both American and Swedish myths were these countries' own histories, even if devoid of factual elements and with sacred quality added. Polish managers did not reach to history for the source of myth because, rich in heroism as it is, it did not offer good examples of effective economic organizations.

All myths reflect certain important social values, maybe those which are most challenged by everyday events. Everyday life in large U.S. corporations hardly provides opportunities for romantic endeavors. Life in Polish organizations is exceedingly romantic, and the positivistic dreams of order and predictability are never fulfilled. Rationality is a very high value in Swedish society, but emotions and organizational politics do not permit achievement of all its high standards.

To all those cultural elements more transitory symbols can be tied, therefore increasing their legitimacy. We can now see how successfully the "propaganda of success" was tied to the "myth of systems," and through it, to the even more persistent "myth of the fatal tendency to anarchy." Ideologies are not, however, the only symbolic expressions present in organizations. Rituals, for example, can be also related to myths, thus gaining in legitimacy, and to ideologies, thus helping to control.

Each myth has supporting rituals, activities having no meaning except symbolic confirmation of what is said in the myth. And so U.S. managers repeat in public how important people are, both at organizational social events and outside the organization. Poles develop very intensive system design activities, and the researchers play a very important role in designing new systems. The Swedes repeat in public utterances about how alive and important their independent administration tradition is.

We can summarize the present discussion on myths and their relation to organizational reality by showing some observed linkages (see Figure 3.1).

As myths help to save important values, organizational control can follow a pattern that is demanded by external contingencies. U.S. corporations are controlled with the use of impersonal systems (action control), as that gives the headquarters better opportunities to deal with the diversity of subordinate units. The multiple form of control in Poland refers to the situation of 1978–80, when the leadership made the "propaganda of success" less and less effective by increasing action control. The Swedish public agencies were, at least during the time when the myth of independence was at the peak of its popularity, controlled mostly by varying inputs of resources from the political side—a version of ecological control.

In the next section we shall move beyond the empirical data to propose a more systematic concept of linkages among culture, organizational symbols, and organizational reality that can be of use in further analysis of ideological control.

CULTURES, SYMBOLIC ACTS, AND ORGANIZATIONS

Man will instinctively try to find meaning and order in a confusing and ambiguous situation, and one "solution" is to "believe" that leaders can deal with uncertainty, the complex and the threatening. We know that other societies "used" the rain dance, the Oracle, the candle, mass and bell, etc. but we have not asked if the plan, the budget, the committee and certain types of social research could be analyzed from the same perspective, as producing an illusion of order and rationality and therefore giving some kind of security

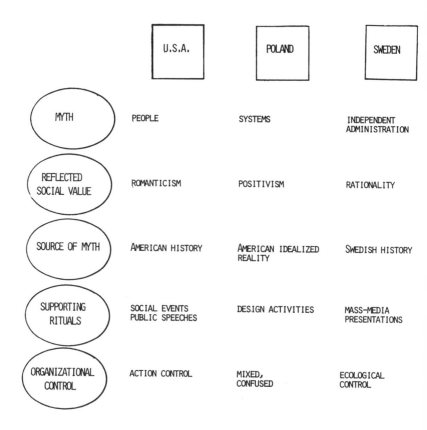

Figure 3.1
Myths, Cultures, Organizations

(and preventing a comparison of certain beliefs against reality). (Olsen 1970, p. 103)

This was written well before the "organizational culture" fad, and since then symbolic organizational acts have been given much more attention. In part, it has helped to introduce the new way of thinking about organizations that Dahl and Olsen postulated. In part, it has contributed to an ever-increasing confusion, in which "culture" is whatever an author wishes it to be, "myth" is any erroneous belief, "ritual" is the same as a routine or any symbolic action, "ideology" is something that must not be found in organizations if they are nice. In some works all these concepts are used interchangeably. This confusion has interesting historical sources: anthropology's long isolation from other social sciences; Marxist (late Marxian) specific treatment of "ideology" (discussed in Chapter 1); a general, powerful encounter of many disciplines (political science, anthropology, sociology, psychology, economics) that for many years lived in blissful isolation from each other and are now forced to enter the same object, a modern organization. But this historical and methodological route to straightening out the confusion, however interesting, is not the only one. An alternative route leads through systematic collection and interpretation of empirical data related to organizations' symbolic activities. The concept of legitimation as an overarching goal for those activities can serve as a general perspective under which various symbolic activities can be analyzed. Another possibility is control, as indicated many a time in our analysis. As legitimation and control in many cases operate in the same direction, we shall assume, for the time being, that they overlap. In reality, they represent two different orientations, proactive and reactive: legitimation is received (if it is given, it becomes control), whereas control is exercised.

Figure 3.2 shows how symbolic acts serve to gain legitimacy and control by creating relationships with the past and the future. Jacobsson and Sahlin-Andersson's (1985) idea that organizations relate to the past and signal the future in order to learn legitimacy is useful here. Myths represent the important events of the past, narrate origins and transformations, and can be evoked in appropriate contexts. Prophecies are similar narrations, but future-oriented: prophecies that come true become myths, and prophets become mythological heroes (Cohen 1969), or at least main narrators. As there are many myths and proph-

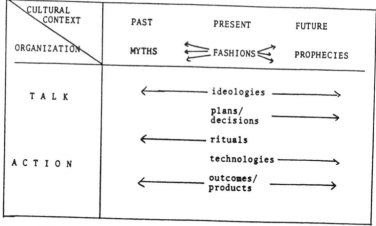

Figure 3.2
Symbolic Acts as Legitimation and Control Devices

ecies available at any point in time, fashions play a selective role, indicating which myths and prophecies are "in" and which are "out."

Symbolic acts also play a linking role between visions (past and future), on the one hand, and reality, on the other. If myths are to compensate for the most acute defects of reality, some linking device is needed. Ideology interprets the reality, gives hope for its change (alluding to a myth or a prophecy), and a recipe for change. On the other hand, faith in a myth can help to resolve the possible contradictions within the ideology as such (Abravanel 1982) or between the ideology and reality. In the latter case, the cultural anchoring substitutes for reality anchoring.

Ideologies are the form of symbolic expression on which the present book focuses. But there are many other symbolic expressions in organizational life:

The use of ritual, ceremonial and pageantry to give legitimacy and propriety to important actions in the life of an association is so widespread in human societies that it should astonish no one to discover that modern democratic societies have also created their own ceremonials. Nor should it surprise that in a community where the democratic ethos is powerful and traditional the rituals take predominantly democratic aspects. (Dahl 1961, p. 112)

Thus, symbolic expressions acquire their role as legitimating and/or controlling devices by relating the organizational present to the past, to the future, or to both. Plans, decisions, and technologies tend to allude to some sort of desired state, a vision, a utopia (on symbolic framings of technologies, see Berg 1985). Rituals, on the other hand, stress tradition. It is quite sensible to expect that those forms which can achieve both, such as ideologies and outcomes, are probably most powerful, both as legitimating and as controlling devices. Also, one should stress that symbolic acts can be, and often are, related to each other, therefore increasing and supporting their legitimacy and controlling power.

Of course, "increase" is not the only direction that organizational phenomena can assume. There are many examples of spectacularly unsuccessful attempts at building linkages between reality and culture, and between various symbols. Sometimes, in the haste to gain anchoring, ideologies are linked to wrong myths and supported by wrong rituals or artifacts. Stites (1985) recalls with amusement the first months after the October Revolution and the attempts of Kerensky's provisional government to anchor the "revolutionary ideology" in something more stable, ending with a czarist flag, a French melody as a national anthem, an Orthodox Church funeral, and a slightly "improved" Byzantine eagle. All connections were wrong, and the combination proved deadly. The Bolsheviks (especially Lunaczarski, the culture commissary) were clever enough to evoke, or perhaps even produce, a myth of "revolution's prehistory." Lunaczarski himself can be seen as a master of the art of symbolic linkages, not in the manipulative and morally doubtful way of Goebbels, but as a true artist. Unfortunately, the heavier modes of control introduced in crisis made his services redundant.

Talk and action can be seen as two main forms that the organizational symbolic act can take. As talk is a "natural" form for ideological control, we shall dedicate the next section to the analysis of organizational, and especially ideological, talk (for linkages between action and, for example, myths, see Gustafsson 1984).

TALK

Talk can be seen as a kind of social action, in the sense that it is an intentional act addressed to social actors (Giddens 1981, 1984; Harré

1981, 1982; Harré and Secord 1976; Jönsson 1982; Sabini and Silver 1982). By the same token, talk can be seen as a subcategory or a special kind of social action—if it is defined as a use of language in an act of communication. Such a definition associates talk with rhetoric, which, however, stresses only formal aspects of talk, and even more with discourse. The latter term, contrary to the rhetoric, stresses mostly the communication aspect: as Barthes says, "*dis-cursus*—originally the action of running here and there, comings and goings, measures taken, 'plots and plans' " (Barthes 1981, p. 3).

Talk, as I said before, is one of the two possible forms in which linkages between culture and organizational symbols, among organizational symbols, and between organizational symbols and organizational reality can be shaped. In such an endeavor three devices can be of great use: labels, metaphors, and platitudes.

Labels

Labels are the most recognized element of organizational talk. The recognition comes initially from political science: labeling, as the linguistic structuring of (social) problems, is one of the most common methods of influence by language.

Political and ideological debate consists very largely of efforts to win acceptance of a particular categorization of an issue in the face of competing efforts in behalf of a different one; but because participants are likely to see it as a dispute either about facts or about individual values, the linguistic (that is, social) basis of perceptions is usually unrecognized. (Edelman 1977, p. 25)

We have seen an (unsuccessful) attempt at labeling when the Polish leadership, in order to repair the ailing legitimacy of the ruling ideology, tried to label the situation in the Polish economy a "crisis." Later on, in Solidarity times (1980–81), the government and Solidarity fought a battle of meanings where labels were of strategic significance (Bialecki 1982; Czarniawska 1986).

Weick points out the important role of labeling in organizations:

Labels carry their own implications for action, and that is why they are so successful in the management of ambiguity. Consider these labels: that is a cost (minimize it), that is a spoilage (reduce it) . . . that is a stupidity (exploit it) and so forth. In each of these instances a label consolidates bits and pieces of data, gives the meaning, suggests appropriate action, implies a diagnosis, and removes ambiguity. (Weick 1985, p. 128)

Successful labeling is clearly one of the keys to power (Smircich and Morgan 1982; Weick 1985). Linguistic artifacts such as labels, metaphors, and platitudes are important tools of power forging. And the first two, especially, are engaged in service of ideologies.

Metaphors

. . . the process of metaphorical conception is a basic mode of symbolism, central to the way in which humans forge their experience and knowledge of the world in which they live. (Morgan 1980, p. 610)

To understand better the role and function of metaphors, it is useful to compare them with factual judgments. Factual judgment is built on a basis coming from the exterior of language, whereas metaphor, which is a semiotic judgment, draws the idea of a possible connection from the interior of language (Eco 1979).

What is different is the amount of time spent in order to produce knowledge. Factual judgments as such die as soon as they are transformed into semiotic judgments. . . . Successful factual judgments are remembered as such only when they become famous ("the famous discovery of Copernicus"). On the other hand, metaphors . . . tend to resist acquisition. If they are inventive (and thus original), they cannot be easily accepted; the system tends not to absorb them. Thus they produce, prior to knowledge, something which, psychologically speaking, we could call "excitation". . . . When faced with metaphor, we sense that it is turning into a vehicle of knowledge, and intuitively . . . we grasp its legitimacy. . . . (Eco 1979, pp. 86–87)

Metaphor is an operation in the course of which "aspects of one object are 'carried over' or transferred to another object, so that the second object is spoken of as if it were the first" (Hawkes 1972, p. 1). Metaphors can be

—Acceptable, when they evoke a desired association but fail to achieve aesthetic power of influence—"organizations as political systems" (Morgan 1980) can be an example of such a metaphor

—Rewarding, when they create a new association—"organizations as garbage cans" (Cohen, March, and Olsen 1972) is a good example of such a metaphor

—Defaulting (deceiving), when it is very hard to discover the association and, when found, it is not really illuminating—"organizations as seesaws" (Hedberg et al. 1976) can, in my opinion, be an example of such a metaphor. Another case of a defaulting metaphor consists, as Eco puts it, in "matching something that our common knowledge has long since matched, and without exciting results" (Eco 1979, p. 4).

With the last example we approach platitudes, but before we move there, let us remain with organizational metaphors for a while longer.

Until recently, metaphors remained in the sphere of theory of literature, semiotics, and hermeneutics. As all of those approached organizational theory (or, rather, when organizational theory became interested in those fields), the metaphor landed in the center of organizational attention. It has been proposed that one could use field metaphors as a tool of comparative analysis of different organizations (Manning 1979), and that major metaphors of organizational theory could be detected from those field metaphors (Morgan 1980). The enthusiasm this task produced has led to a formulation of a serious warning against a metaphor overdose (Pinder and Bourgeois 1982). My intention is to focus on metaphors of the field, those used by the actors, with the purpose of understanding their role in promoting, spreading, and accepting an ideology. I would like to point out that they are more than decorative figures of speech (see also Morgan 1983), and that, being symbolic expressions, they are at the same time specifically instrumental.

Metaphors serve a very important function in the spreading of a new ideology. They establish new meanings by fitting them into imagination-stimulating messages. In this sense, their role consists in reducing the uncertainty produced by the encounter with the new: they refer to something that is better known than the object of the metaphor. They can be seen as shortcuts in explanation, as they try to evoke a single image that encompasses the whole idea. They are also easily acceptable, because their "decorative" characteristics answer the need for color and a touch of life in the otherwise somber organizational reality. This can explain the startling fact that, as Thompson puts it, following Percy (1961), a metaphor "is often most effective when it is most 'wrong' " (Thompson 1980, p. 233). It is the metaphor's expressive power, and not its reflective power, that is most important (Geertz 1964).

Platitudes

In literary criticism, platitudes are considered to be a defect, an error in the art of creative writing or speaking. They can be seen as verbal rituals, utterances whose meaning is entirely symbolic. They do not denote concrete things or happenings: they point to certain other meanings and ideas, and their repetitive character makes this link very obvious and easy to understand. These characteristics suggest an obvious linkage between platitudes and rituals, between the present and the past. Indeed, platitudes are not typical for expressing ideologies.

However, ideologies always contain at least one part (the vision) that is strikingly new, no matter how well anchored. Sometimes all three parts (the representation, the vision, and the program) are shockingly new, as in our next case. In that perspective an observation made by therapists is of a value: that in verbal interaction the role of platitudes can be completely different from that in a literary text. The most significant role of platitudes is their facilitation of an interaction by reduction of uncertainty (Hendricks 1984). In other words, in an interaction filled with tension due to a high level of uncertainty, a platitude serves to reduce this tension by pointing out a certain common ground and certain values that are shared by all the participants.

Platitude seems to be the opposite of metaphor, but actually they both fulfill the same function in a different way: they reduce uncertainty by relating the unknown to a better known (metaphor) or to a very well known (platitude). The relation between them is continuous, and their precise place on the continuum depends on the experience of the receiver: what for some is a platitude is for others a daring metaphor. This statement became especially true for me when I offered my study on ideological control in Swedish municipalities (Chapter 5) for my Swedish colleagues' critique. What I considered a rich field metaphor sounded like a platitude to them, as it was apparently coined many years before I came to Sweden. On the other hand, what to me sounded like a platitude was often a metaphor to them.

As stated above, the role of platitudes at the side of ideological control is only secondary: they ease tensions produced by farfetched metaphors and shocking ideologies. Yet this secondary role is equally important: like safety valves, platitudes diminish tension when it builds up too high.

SUMMARY

The analysis of the phenomenon of ideological control introduced many concepts concerning other symbolic elements found in organizations and outside organizations. Earlier studies on organizational control contributed to a better insight into the role of organizational myths. Further discussion led to identification of myths, fashions, and prophecies present in organizational environments, which can be seen as elements of the cultural context of organizing. Inside organizations, ideologies, rituals, and also decisions and technologies in their symbolic meaning are supported by relations to this cultural context (and, in their turn, contribute to the maintenance of the context).

This continuous process of relating organizational symbols to the cultural context of organizing (and back) constitutes a significant ingredient of legitimation and control processes. A successful coupling of internal and external symbols increases legitimacy (both for the group of actors who perform this operation in front of the rest of the organization's members, and for the organization as seen from the outside). Increased legitimacy facilitates control, and effective control increases legitimacy.

With this set of analytical tools we shall move to the analysis of the next empirical case of ideological control.

4

Ideological Control in a Company

SVENSKT FÖRETAG AB: HISTORY AND IDEOLOGY

Svenskt Företag AB (SF AB), a manufacturer in the processing industry, is held by a company owned by the Swedish state. Its sales for
1985 and 1986 were around 1 billion Swedish kronor, and it employed
almost 1,000 people in its headquarters, four divisions, and five sales
regions. Almost 85 percent of sales were exports. SF AB was very
successful until 1974, when, as a result of an ill-advised allocation
decision and a disadvantageous business cycle, its profits began to
diminish and it suffered losses. When the decline was at its bottom, a
new president was called in (1978). In 1983 I conducted a study on
control issues in relation to top management (how the headquarters
controls general managers and their units).

The main source of data was 17 open interviews with the top executives of SF AB. These were complemented by analysis of various
organizational documents. The analysis, performed according to the
"grounded theory" approach (Glaser and Strauss 1974), revealed, among

other things, that ideological control was the main mode of control at the top levels of SF AB. The president said:

> I used ideological control immediately after we started, in the second week. I believe in Goebbels' theory, that if you repeat something often enough, it finally becomes true. Of course, truth is a relative concept, but if you repeat something, and you say it, and you say it, and you use every kind of means to get the message through, finally people start to believe it. It is a long, tedious process, but you have got to be firm about it.

As the employees remember it, at the end of 1977 the atmosphere was very gloomy in all parts of the corporation:

> It was a mess. Most people believed that SF AB could be closed down any day. But most people thought that state ownership is a guarantee of security, so they stayed. . . . And also, we thought that the owners had just invested so much money in us that they would not dare to close us down. . . .

The new president was appointed on February 1, 1978, and at the beginning of March he held a meeting with all executives. What the new president offered them was a powerful catharsis. People in SF AB knew "that there was something wrong with them, but they did not know what." So they were told.

> It was very frustrating, this . . . almost questioning your existence within the company. But it acted as a very powerful shake-up: people understood that one most not be here just as an employed person, but one has to contribute whether one is going to stay here or not. And the threat became real; nobody thought of the state ownership anymore, but: is this part of the company going to remain? For the first time we understood that, even if we are a state-owned company, they are not going to put up any money just to let us live. And I think that was very healthy.

The diagnosis, the first part of the new ideology, consisted in an almost brutal confrontation with the economic reality, and in removing the remnants of the old ideology. Although SF AB had been steered mostly by ecological control (new resources were continuously poured into divisions or units that were to expand), as in all organizations, some elements of all modes of control were present. There were at least three ideological elements. First, the company's size was valuable. The old leadership was expansion-minded, and expansion was seen purely in terms of size. Second, the previous leadership was characterized as (in one formulation) "by a childish fascination with new technologies," and there were several people who shared this fascination. But this was hardly an ideology to motivate salesmen, who were an important part of the company, and, all in all, it is not a particularly attractive ideology for managers. Engineers and technical people are fascinated with technologies. Managers tend to treat technologies instrumentally. Third, the ideology of the owner was at that time to use the company as a "tool for industrial policy": a means of fighting unemployment and stimulating industrial development in the northern part of the country. The mission of the company was therefore defined more in political than in economic terms.

All this must come to an end, said the new president. There are no resources for continuing expansion: investments must be stopped. Technology should be the instrument for sales, and not a plaything for engineers. And, finally, the owners had changed their ideology and wanted a profitable company, not a tool for industrial policy.

Of course, the offer was not only negative. The positive element in it consisted of a new identity that was offered to the company's executives. Before 1978, SF AB was perceived as "an emulsion with no profile, no character," and its managers, especially its sales managers, felt as if they were "floating in this emulsion without an aim." The new ideology was a chance, an offer, a definition of a place—and it was accepted with gratitude, turning into involvement, turning into commitment that was demonstrated in actions. "People worked very hard to prove that their job was *not* needed. . . . "

And it was this motivational anchorage, as we shall see through the discussion, that decided the strength of the appeal of the new ideology. As Schein (1983) notes, the basic condition for the acceptance of a new element of a culture is that this element contains a solution to a problem the group is facing.

What was the attraction, or rather, what was the vision proposed by the new ideology? As the company's corporate policy formulated it, "to be world champions at what we are doing, to be one of Sweden's most attractive companies."

These two overarching goals had several more concrete formulations. First of all, profitability must become a main measure of the company's success. And profitability was defined not so much in economic as in moral terms. As one of the general managers said:

The first thing I asked my closest managers was: do you want your neighbor to pay your salary? Forget everything else. The only thing that is honorable is to pay your own salary, so let's work with profit, let's work on how to make profit. . . .

To be world champions requires a competitive strength within the world market, and this requires expansion, not in terms of size but in terms of scope. SF AB should be growing like a mushroom culture, capturing new niches by virtue of remaining small and highly adaptable: " . . . let there be many small, beautiful things spread all over the world and adjusted to the country in which they live. . . . "

This adaptability calls for change as a mark of the company's activities: such as the formulation used in the corporate policy brochure. Or, as one of the general managers expressed it:

. . . you asked me if this organization that we've got today, if this will fit when we will be 10 times or 20 times bigger—I don't think so. I don't think we will work the same way, I don't think that you will find the same people, and I certainly do not think that we will have the same culture as we have today. Look at old companies, they started with one business idea but they have turned several times. They haven't got the same business or product because the world is still changing all the time. You always live with change. . . .

Change was important for another goal: becoming a model Swedish company. Or maybe even more than that. Here it is formulated by the president:

. . . what I want of SF AB, in a few years' time, is to become a vision of how a Swedish company can transform itself. How a Swedish company could really become very successful. You could say a master plan or some kind of example to follow. Because I think that everything has to be transformed from below, not from above, in a society. The politicians, they just listen to what they hear and they try to do certain things, but the way to really influence the environment in a country is to start an experiment, start doing something, prove that it is successful, and then others will follow. And that is what I am doing here. That is my overriding ambition. Take just one example: as we say, we have a codetermination, we are now pushing self-determination. The logic is very clear. If people get used to self-determination in the company, why would they not ask for that in the society as a whole? Less power for the politicians, more power for the individuals.

The important aspects of this model building were success (as defined by profits), modernity (technological and organizational), and democracy.

The two main ways of achieving these visions were through a change in organizational ways of functioning and through a change of people. We shall discuss both of them at greater length, but before we do so, we shall consider the ties between the proposed ideology and its broader context.

The ideology, which can be called "the dream of an ideal company," was quite obviously anchored in two national cultures at the same time: "people as profit makers" was of American origin, and "democracy and self-determination" was Swedish. As a matter of fact, SF AB was a bilingual company: top managers used the two languages interchangeably. The purposeful use of English was of a great importance for ideological talk, as we shall see later. The vision part of the ideology promised to become what is best in both cultures, in relation to business and organization. The reality anchorage was very strong, thanks to three major events: the fact that the owners agreed to cover some major losses from the past, in order to give the company a fresh start; the devaluation of the Swedish krona; and a major technological innovation patented by the company. The last loss occurred in 1978; since then, sales and profits have grown steadily.

But most important, in my opinion, was the psychological appeal, or the motivational anchorage. All top managers became believers: they perceived the ideology as their personal change for growth, development, and success. This impact of the ideology was visible through all its aspects and uses.

CHANGING THE ORGANIZATION

Many organizational-change devices and innovations introduced in SF AB can be seen as means for action control. What I would like to show, however, is that even action-control situations contain strong

OPERATIONS	STRATEGIC DEVELOPMENT
Control	Development
Closed	Open
Defensive	Offensive
Check-up	Goals/Visions
Security	Freedom/Uncertainty
Efficiency	Effectiveness
Program	Trial and error
Evaluation	Understanding

Figure 4.1
Operations and Strategic Development Organizations at SF AB

ideological messages and that some ways of control that apparently aim at action are actually symbolic and, as such, their main function is to support the ideology and not to produce concrete behaviors.

The double organization (Operations and Strategic Development) can be an example of such a device. The two organizations were to be characterized, according to the policy formulation, by the values shown in Figure 4.1.

The Operations organization was structured according to more or less conventional hierarchy principles. Strategic Development was headed by the Development Committee, supported by the Scientific Advisory Board, and organized into thematic "strategy groups." Most top managers, apart from their line responsibilities, had responsibility within strategic groups. The creation of the Strategic Development organization aimed at pooling creativity and preventing short-term thinking, but it was also used as a source of renewal for the ideology, as a means of propagating it, and as a symbol for it.

This opportunity for strategic thinking helped managers to identify with the dominant ideology. General managers were encouraged to develop and propose mini visions of their own, to appropriate certain parts of the ideology.

. . . you have or create a vision of what you want to do a couple of years ahead, and from that you work out a development frame for the nearest five years, and then you make your plans according to it. Because if you don't put a vision of what you want to do in front of yourself and your people, you will never make it.

These visions were publicly reviewed and recorded, a procedure that effectively built up commitment:

Every year we run a two- or three-day strategy seminar session where we use videotape. What happens is that all of us first review what we said last year, we look at the videotape, then we have some general discussions about strategic issues for SF AB and what we want to do about them, and then the last day we make new commitments for the next 12-month period on videotape.

This public commitment made managers identify strongly with their visions. In fact, I was struck by the missionary spirit that was very apparent from the first encounters. As in my previous studies, I expected to ask managers questions that were relevant to me, but each of them would come to the interview with a portfolio of transparencies, and before I could start my questions, I had to listen to an exposition of their missions. The congruence of the message sent by the top people in the headquarters and the general managers was unusually high, yet general managers did not create an impression of simple repetition. It was this feeling of a mission to fulfill that was their main reward, in the light of limits put on managerial remuneration by the Swedish tax system:

As you have been participating in setting up those development frames or visions of what you or you together with somebody else want to do, it becomes very important, at least for me, to fulfill those things, and to do such things is a big satisfaction in itself. You expect from it a reasonable financial contribution, but for me it is not the money that is the important thing. It is to be able to work together with somebody, to develop something new that was not there from the beginning.

In that sense managers were both believers and missionaries: the ideology was used to control them, but their full acceptance of its message and their willingness to propagate it made it more into a self-control. It also increased the probability of the ideology's penetrating downward, an unusual event, as the ideologies addressed to the managerial and/or professional level usually remain there (Clegg and Dunkerley 1980).

An interesting device, at first sight strictly instrumental, was a matrix structure (production divisions and sales regions) and a system of internal prices. It was interesting mostly because this was the only issue that was really controversial. Headquarters was very enthusiastic about the solution, which was to bolster the competitive spirit and to reinforce the importance of profitability. Some managers claimed that the device was very useful as a socialization means, as a way of teaching the new ideology, but as familiarity with the new ways of acting grew, the solution become redundant. Others perceived it in the opposite way: the internal pricing was very difficult at the beginning and its usefulness increased with growing familiarity. Still others claimed that the main secret was not to treat it literally and to establish the rules of cooperation (between divisions and regions) on a personal basis. Yet another group seemed to see the use of internal pricing as a learning device: it allowed simulation of the "true" market inside the company.

All these perspectives can be reconciled if we interpret the matrix structure and internal pricing as rituals supporting the ideology. The solution symbolizes two important elements of the ideology: modernity (matrix structure was, at that time, the hottest news in organizational design) and competitive power. In that sense those who said they did not take it literally best understood the ritualistic function of this organizational form. The forms were mostly pretexts or symbols expressing a certain way of thinking: their controlling role was minimal.

The president formulated it thus:

It is all based on the basic premise: that business is people, period. Our systems here are to free up people, while retaining a certain amount of coordination. But we do not coordinate just for the fun of coordinating: we retain the minimum amount of coordination that is necessary for the organization to work. If you have wrong rules of the game, you may induce the behavior that is not desirable, and that is why the systems are very important; but when we design systems here, we do it with the ultimate purpose of freeing up people. To give people more authority. That is the general idea. . . . I would be happy to have no systems at all, if everybody was competent enough to think for themselves, and act in a mature way, but unfortunately I know that this is not so in human life, so let us then design the systems so as to minimize undesirable effects, but maximize the authority of individuals. Right?

The above statement is a reconciliation of the ''system myth'' with the ''people myth'' but puts the ultimate weight on the latter. The ''people myth'' was the main myth SF AB's ideology was anchored in, and it was through people that the main changes were to occur. If the previous case, that of the Polish economy, should be summarized in its ''how-to-do-it'' aspect, it was a ''success through systems.'' Here we have a ''success through people'' case.

CHANGING PEOPLE

Another memory of the first meeting relates it thus:

. . . he talked two hours . . . he said that we could see from the results that what we were doing was wrong, so we must change everything. Every mind shall be changed. We start now, and next week we shall have a new manager in every position.

And that was, indeed, what happened:

. . . we changed the whole board of directors, we changed the whole of the executive management, we changed every single divisional manager, every marketing director, every production director, every regional director, and the whole group in five years.

After the physical change of people was completed, further socialization could start. The personnel development program was of high priority at SF AB. It has followed a certain philosophy, as the president explained:

There are two basic philosophies about development. One is the so-called engineering philosophy and the other is the gardener philosophy. If you have an engineering philosophy about development, you look upon people as pieces of metal that you put into a lathe and then into a grinding machine and then into a lathing machine and then you put them into the oven to harden the surface, and then perhaps you grind them again, and finally you have a piece that fits perfectly into the organization chart. The only mistake with that particular philosophy is that it is poorly wrought. There is no way that I can develop you, and there is no way you can develop me. You develop yourself if you want to do it and if you feel inclined to do it. If the environment is such that you feel that you want to develop yourself.

Therefore, it is much better to take a gardener attitude. You look upon the company as a garden with plants all around. Then it is the responsibility of the gardener to walk through this garden and water the plants, give them a little extra soil, perhaps fertilizer sometimes. Perhaps one plant is sitting in the shade and needs more sun, so you pick it up and move it into the sun, and someone in the sun should be put in the shade. And perhaps somebody in sandy soil should be moved into some other kind of soil, and sometimes you have to remove some undesirable plants that hinder the growth of the others. If you look upon the company this way, then things start to happen.

This "gardening philosophy" was put into operational terms in the executive training and development program. The first stage contained the following seminars:

- Decentralization: how advanced is decentralization in SF AB? Do we live according to what we preach?
- Leadership philosophy: what is SF AB's leadership philosophy? (Purpose: to popularize the company's leadership philosophy.)
- Organization: how is our organization functioning? What changes are necessary?
- Cooperation: how well do we cooperate in our unit? in the whole company?
- Individualism and cooperation: how to be independent and yet cooperate?
- Opportunities to be creative in the company.

The first seminar contained a thorough indoctrination into the ideology. The second contained a course in transaction analysis, career counseling, and smaller courses in increased assertiveness and personal efficiency. The third seminar offered a communications course, knowledge and information sharing, and a course in building a functional network. The fourth offered development of pride in one's work, a course in motivation, a course in constructive criticism, and a course in public presentations. The fifth seminar contained a course in relationships, a decision-making course, and a positive negotiating course. The further perspective foresaw focus on self-assertion, meditation, and creativity training. Additionally, the company paid the fee if an executive wished to participate in EST, sensitivity training, or any other personality development training. The participation must take place after working hours but, I was told (no official data exist), many executives took the opportunity. SF AB offered its executives an opportunity to change their lives and personalities, to develop, quite literally, a new identity.

The main goal was, of course, to recruit and socialize an adequate group of top managers or, as the official formulation put it, to "improve the depth of management":

We need to be able to develop more general manager types in SF AB, so that our expansion will not be hampered by lack of good people. And I think it is also important to bring people up in the organization, in other words, to recruit good, sharp people rather early in their careers, and then let them have a chance to grow in the corporation. Because so much of our way of doing things has to do with management philosophy, the way of looking at things, so, if they have been working for our competitor for ten years, they will not be fit to work for us, I mean, their whole value system has to be radically changed. . . .

This ideology of achieving organizational change through personal change reached further than the "depth of management." One of the respondents informed me that "firing people is obsolete in the '80's," and to corroborate his thesis related a case of a subordinate manager whose performance was unsatisfactory and did not improve in spite of numerous discussions and evaluations. The employee was sent for a defense mechanisms test, as his superior put it, "to find his strengths and weaknesses and to find out what he should actually work with." The superior's opinion was that the best thing for the employee in question would be to buy a tobacco shop, but he (the superior) wanted a third party to enter the discussion:

Firing people is a cynical and easy way out, quick and dirty. It is a sign of incompetence, it is a way you get rid of a manager who couldn't live up to the goals that you decided upon. Instead of discussing the matter of firing him after 18 years in this company, it is a discussion about how to develop him, for his remaining 8 years, how to help him to make a success of his life, so that he, as a human being, can be proud of what he is doing.

What are the results of such a psychologically oriented ideological approach? Brainwashing or personal fulfillment? Opinions differ. Salaman (1979) speaks of "psychologism" as a type of organizational ideology and notes that, with the aid of such an ideology:

Organizational members are encouraged to see themselves as organizational resources which require constant scrutiny and adjustment. . . .

The importance of [management training courses] for influencing members' attitudes and motivation must be stressed. Training occupies an increasing number of expert organizational personnel, and most members will be sent on courses of some sort at some stage of their organizational careers. The function of these courses is to adjust organizational members to organizational demands and realities; to encourage members to gain "insight" into themselves, their colleagues and the organization ("insight" of a rather limited sort, usually); to inform members about the organization, and to develop new skills. They achieve insidious control. (Salaman 1979, p. 203)

But that was not a dominant perception of the managers at SF AB. They felt proud and distinguished by having the opportunity for personal development. The president's gardening philosophy could not have found a better response than the one below:

You know, every flower needs its own little glass house, with the soil and the temperature and the humidity and everything like that. The president creates a very good glass house for me, and that is enough.

That perception, formulated more or less metaphorically, was common in the headquarters and in divisions/regions situated in Sweden. However, a visit to a foreign subsidiary provided a different picture. The managers of the subsidiary were happy with their communication and interpersonal skills, and considered communication or self-assertiveness courses as possibly threatening the individual's integrity. The courses' optional character allowed the managers to ignore the headquarters' offer, and the headquarters did not insist, considering distance and language difficulties (some courses were in Swedish).

A question arises: how typical is the case of SF AB? Do managers accept or resent psychological channels of ideology propagation? It is doubtful whether a sensible test could be developed to verify this issue in a reliable way. We can turn, though, to another case of striking similarity.

"EMMABODA IN OUR HEARTS"

Per-Olof Berg relates an amazing example of organizational development in his analysis of changes at Emmaboda Glasverk, a glass factory in southeastern Sweden (Berg 1979).

In 1968, the president (and owner) of the company had learned from a consultant company about a novelty in management training, called sensitivity training. He and one of the consultants went to the United States to participate in such training. They returned with two decisions made: that the consulting company would run an experimental program of that kind in Sweden, and that the experiment would take place at Emmaboda Glasverk. Very much like the president of SF AB, who considered his participation in EST the most profound experience of his life, the president of Emmaboda Glasverk was totally convinced:

I came home filled to the brim with this, and started up in my usual way. Everyone in the company should attend sensitivity training. It is a way to get people to communicate in a new and different way. (Berg 1979, p. 91)

The consultant group performed a survey study that showed the need for improved communication; an experimental session was organized and positively evaluated, and the first training was to take place in the Canary Islands. The results were profound: the training was a profound and powerful experience for all the participants, and at the same time isolated them from the rest (it was a group of about 25 managers).

The aftermath of the training was the growing importance of personnel issues in the company. Career counseling (for top management) was initiated by the president. At the same time, the remaining group of managers pressed for the continuation of the sensitivity training. It was done, but not in such an attractive location, and with an inexperienced trainer. It was not a total failure, but neither was it a success. Nevertheless, the general impression among the members of top management was that the sensitivity training method was effective.

We were very profitable . . . had a high-quality product development, etc., and there were no clouds in the sky. The future looked bright, and everything was happiness. We had comradeship and an open atmosphere, as if we belonged to an exclusive club. . . .

All external contacts said: "I see—you are from EGV. That's the company with the funny advertisement campaigns ["Emmaboda in our hearts" was the most famous of them] who are working with sensitivity training." (Berg 1979, p. 109)

The third training session took place with participation of blue-collar union representatives. The participants were very positive, even if the union representatives had serious problems explaining the idea to their unions.

The president progressed furthest. He partly withdrew from the company, separated from his wife, and started to experiment with alternative life-styles. One of his projects, called Man Alive, aimed at a "total integration of society, employees, family, and company" (Berg 1979, p. 112), and was to include the top management of Emmaboda Glasverk.

However, while the president and many of the managers were deeply immersed in the process of personal and interpersonal changes, the shrinking market and the increasing technological competition required positive, quick decisions of a strategic character. Nobody was in a position to make them. As the external threat grew, so did the internal feeling of helplessness and lack of direction. Emmaboda Glasverk was sold and then reorganized, to plunge into a decline from which it did not emerge.

My point here is not to analyze causal relationships between what Berg calls a "cultural revolution" at Emmaboda Glasverk and the later fate of the company. The above presentation concerns only one aspect of the company's functioning, relevant as a possible comparison with SF AB. A striking similarity that is, in my opinion, partly misleading, is the figure of a charismatic leader. If the president of Emmaboda Glasverk was depicted by many as a despot, nevertheless he was obviously very attractive as a role model and object of identification. This was also the case with SF AB's president. As one of the respondents recalled, at the first meeting of the managerial session held outside the company, all managers of SF AB arrived in business suits, to be greeted by the president in a sweater and corduroy trousers. On the following day, everybody was sporting sweaters and jeans, many in the same colors as the president's. Idealizing transference, Kets de Vries and Miller (1984) tell us, occurs quite frequently in organizations.

But a charismatic leader, although evidently helpful in propagating an ideology, is not absolutely necessary. We shall see in the next case that ideological control is possible with a group or diffused leadership. What lurks behind the facade of a charismatic leader is one crucial difference and one crucial similarity. The difference lies in the fact that the president of Emmaboda Glasverk had no organization-relevant ideology to offer. His ideology concerned life-style and life values. The president of SF AB had a business ideology that offered the managers a new identity in their role as managers.

The similarity between the two cases—and, indeed, the main reason why Emmaboda's history was related here—is that both presidents invited their managers to change their personalities, their egos—at the expense of and for the good of the company. Such an offer, when coercive, can be seen as an example of total control. And yet the managers at Emmaboda Glasverk who did not participate in the first sensitivity training felt punished! On the other hand, such an offer has been made in many companies and in many places since 1968. However, the reaction was usually mixed: some saw it as an opportunity; some, as a threat. A common positive response of the whole group seems to indicate a commonly felt problem to which the chosen approach offers a solution. A great deal is said and written about Swedish communication problems, and individuals tend to accept it self-accusingly, believing that this is a personal and cultural defect (Daun 1984).

Such a statement must be elaborated upon in order to avoid an impression of hasty and stereotypical judgments concerning cultural differences. I do not claim that communication problems are a part of Swedish culture; I claim that such a self-perception is common in the Swedish culture. As to the "objective" differences, a study on national differences in extraversion and neuroticism (Lynn and Hampson 1975) places Sweden among the "healthiest" nations—extravert and low on neuroticism. This is not, however, a popular perception. But even the latter is divided on many issues, depending on whether we deal with an insider's or an outsider's perspective (Forss 1987).

My observation is built neither on an objective study of differences nor on a subjective perception. It was my respondents who spoke about themselves and other people as having problems with interpersonal communication (with the exception of the foreign subsidiary, where the respondents both stated that their communication skills were satisfactory and insinuated that their Swedish colleagues' were not). The formulations differed: very often it was "shyness," a personality trait ("the supervisors have to live up to a leader's role, they have to get away from their shyness . . . ''), sometimes an avoidance of conflict and therefore of confrontation and direct feedback, or, as Daun (1984) puts it, a cultural norm that forbids expression of personal judgments and puts an exaggerated weight on verbal utterances.

If we accept this reasoning, the ideology proposed by the new leader of SF AB contained a powerful "psychological package" in the sense that

- Its diagnosis served as a cathartic experience for the frustrated managers of SF AB: it was seen as bitter but true, and therefore bringing relief
- Its vision offered an attractive new identity of a successful, American-style manager
- Its program promised personal development achieved through optimizing the organization.

As stated before, cultural and reality anchorages were also present, although not so visible. The additional example of Emmaboda Glasverk indicates the ties and connections between different types of anchorages: in both cases the motivational anchorage could be seen as supported by a deeper cultural anchorage. Emmaboda Glasverk's history shows, like the case of the Polish economy, the devastating results of loss of the reality anchorage. Ideologies never faithfully portray the reality, but too big a gap ruins their appeal.

IDEOLOGICAL TALK

As the ideology at SF AB was based mainly on the motivational anchorage, the identification of the managers was so far-reaching that the ideology functioned almost as a means of self-control. The target was reached: the new ideology was accepted and internalized. However, both in the propagating phase and in the phase of internalization, talk was put to efficient use.

In the first place, as mentioned before, SF AB was a bilingual company. All top managers were expected to communicate fluently in English (or rather American); most company documents were in both languages, and some training sessions were held in English. This had a very practical purpose: a company planning an expansion to English-speaking countries has a need for English-speaking executives. But it was more than that: the additional language allowed the combination of labeling with metaphor building. Some labels, chosen because of their exotic quality, became metaphors by the fact that they were untranslatable. One such example was ''gumption,'' which was understood, I was told, as ''psychological energy'' and was used as a personal development goal, to be evaluated in career counseling sessions.

Apart from introducing the second language, the president was successful in coining metaphors: the ''gardening attitude'' and the ''hothouse'' metaphors were mentioned by many respondents. One must stress that the president was very conscious of the fact that ideological control was the dominant mode of control and of the role that talk plays in exerting it.

The role of embellishing ideological talk was also given to the consultants. SF AB bought, lock, stock, and barrel, a set of metaphors from an American consulting company, and my respondents, much to the despair of the person who transcribed the interviews, talked about ''milking cash cows,'' ''watching out for wildcats,'' ''predicting stars,'' and establishing ''normal pictures.''

SUMMARY

The case of SF AB confirmed the importance of cultural and reality anchorages for the effective use of ideological control but also introduced a new element: a motivational anchorage. Ideology is accepted—and it must be accepted, at least by some people to some extent, if it is to be used for legitimating and controlling purposes—when it answers some important needs or wishes of people to whom it is addressed.

Individual needs and wishes can, however, hardly be the target of organizational control. We are discussing social processes that are typical for organizations, and in order to integrate individual motivations so as to produce a social action, a social factor is necessary. The cultural context can be such a factor. The social character of motivation is not often dealt with by psychology, so there is not much theory to fall back on. The empirical studies show quite clearly, however, the importance of the cultural context in transforming individual motivations into social action.

5

Ideological Control in Local Governments

THE BACKGROUND OF THE STUDY

The late 1970s and the early 1980s were marked by a wave of experiments in Swedish local governments, aiming at a decentralization of political and administrative activities.

Submunicipal boards were historically the first form of decentralization, and consisted of advisory organs in districts of a municipality. These local organs were supposed to reflect the political situation of a district. Hence every district board could have a different majority, provided the chairperson represented the political majority at the central municipal level. The original idea was that boards should be directly elected, but before that issue was finally settled, it became clear that lack of decision rights and, above all, of economic resources made boards rather ornamental units.

Submunicipal committees (SMCs) followed the idea of the boards and extended it from a purely political to an organizational one. Committees assumed responsibility for social welfare, schools, and recreation in a given district, for example. They were to be directly elected, or at least they ought to reflect the voting profile of a district, but no municipality has exploited this opportunity to date (Amnå et al. 1985).

The vagueness of these descriptions is not accidental. The forms were very amorphous and were to be given content by every municipality individually, in accordance with suggestions of the Local Democracy Committee (LDC).

The LDC was called to life in 1977 by the bourgeois government. In 1979 it presented conclusions containing both proofs of necessity and blueprints for change (*Ds KN* 1979; p. 10).

The central government encouraged decentralization experiments in 1979, but even earlier, in 1977, the municipality of Örebro decided to start theirs. Two other local governments followed in 1979, in close cooperation with both Örebro and LDC. All three decided to introduce SMCs and their attempts took a distinct form after 1980, when the Local Bodies Act was enforced. Experiments spread, and enthusiasm grew. The biggest Swedish daily, *Dagens Nyheter,* reported on April 22, 1985, that 19 municipalities had already introduced SMCs, about 20 had made a decision to start experimenting, 30 others were still investigating the issue, and several others had decided to introduce other forms of decentralization. It was then that our study started.

The previous research results failed to provide a comprehensive frame of reference that would permit an a priori structuring of data collection and analysis. The empirical study was therefore designed along explorative lines, aiming to describe an attempt at an organizational change. Both historical (dynamic) and static approaches were used; the respondents were asked to describe the history of decentralization as their personal experience, and the current shape of control processes as seen from their perspective.

As none of the existing theories was complete enough to formulate an a priori model, the task was theory building rather than theory verification (Glaser and Strauss 1974). The sampling, data collection, and data analysis basically followed the ''grounded theory'' approach (Glaser and Strauss 1974). The starting point was one of the municipalities with the longest experience with SMC reform. The next choice, made on the assumption of minimizing differences, was a municipality similar in size, tradition, and location, also with a relatively advanced reform attempt but experimenting with different sectors (which was the main variation in the contents of the reform). Study of the two allowed the formulation of a first version of a grounded theory and therefore narrowed further investigations to the uncertain issues.

Maximizing differences was then the aim, and the next object was a municipality of a distinctly different size (much larger) and just beginning the reform. The final object was a municipality of the same size (large) but with no current plans to introduce the reform. The size and contents of reform were chosen as the main grounds for minimizing or maximizing differences, as they were shown important in other studies (Dente and Regonini 1980). On the other hand, the most comprehensive Swedish report (Amnå et al. 1985) indicated that neither the financial nor the political situation was an important differentiating factor. We also had access to the secondhand interview data from a fifth municipality, smallest in size and experimenting with different forms of decentralized committees. As the study was meant as neither an advertisement nor an evaluation of the reform, anonymity was preserved.

The main technique was that of a semistructured interview, adapted to the needs of a growing body of theory. Another method, used unsystematically, was that of observation. We were allowed to observe the meetings of SMCs which are not open to the public. Document analysis was a significant part of our data collection and focused on internal documents (letters, protocols, budgets) and external documents such as information leaflets and course materials. Finally, we completed the data by content analysis of the newspapers. We concentrated on one of the central newspapers, with some unsystematic scanning of local press. Anders Forssell and the author collected the data.

In sum, the entire analysis aimed at a reconstruction of an interdisciplinary picture, a social representation of the reform told by those who took part in it.

CHOOSING A FRAME OF REFERENCE

The official utterances presented the reform as decentralization of Swedish local governments. The results showed, however, that there was no basis for speaking about *the* decentralization of Swedish local governments. It was *a* decentralization, as there were, and are, many others, and its proper name was Submunicipal Committee reform.

The most pervasive element was that of introducing ideological control as a dominant control mode in at least some part of a local government, and therefore the ideological control perspective was chosen as a main perspective in analyzing the present study.

The choice was reinforced by the fact that the ideological control perspective seemed to be a frame of reference used by many respondents to explain most of the phenomena encountered. They often used expressions like "ideological" and "religious" while speaking about the reform; they mentioned "ideologues," "philosophers," and "bishops"; and they spoke about "ideologies" and "creeds."

At the same time, this frame of reference turned out to be the least selective and the most comprehensive, allowing for many other interpretations that could be seen as supportive or competitive ideologies. This comprehensiveness is very important in this particular case, as SMC reform was many things at the same time and, above all, it was a different process for different actors. This was, in fact, one of the most pervasive results of the study: there was no issue on which everybody, or at least a majority, could agree, even within the same municipality. So-called facts proved to be relative: who proposed the reform; when it happened, into how many parts the municipality would be divided; whether the economic situation was good or bad; whether citizens were interested in technical or social matters. All these issues were the subject of the most conflicting statements and judgments. There was no one picture of the reform, and there was no single conclusion or recommendation that could be made as a result of the study.

Hence, it has been decided to treat the current SMC reform of Swedish local governments as a case of ideological control, a case where an ideology served to introduce an organizational change. The following description aims at presenting the contents of the ideology (what?), the structure produced (who?), and the ongoing processes (how?).

THE IDEOLOGY: DEMOCRACY VIA DECENTRALIZATION

An ideology is a set of ideas that describe how things are, how they should be, and how to achieve the desired state. It is used as a justification of the leaders' behavior and as a framework of shared meaning that can be used as a basis for the actions of the followers. The set of ideas that is in focus in this chapter can be called democracy via decentralization.

The ideology of democracy via decentralization was formed and used on two levels: the central level (the Social Democratic [SD] Party and the government, especially the Ministry of Civil Affairs) and the local level (local governments). The beginnings go back to the late 1970s, but the report of the government's Investigation Committee was published in August 1985. Under the headline "Ge folk ökat inflytande" (Give people more influence), *Dagens Nyheter* of August 2, 1985, reported on the new developments as follows:

The municipal bureaucracy is now to embrace its "clients" and "consumers." Submunicipal committees will bring decisions closer to citizens. Service will match needs, for example, extended working hours. "Ordinary people" can participate when politicians and officers determine municipal services. This is how things are going to be if the Government follows up the "democracy proposal."

The central level propagated its ideology by introducing it as a topic for debate in the mass media, by initiating and reviewing research reports, and by means of internal party information. In support of these efforts, the Swedish Association of Local Authorities organized a series of seminars in Örebro, the "model" municipality, for all local governments that were interested in the experiment. Foreign guests were invited to visit Örebro and to learn about current research on decentralization.

Before we leave the central level, one thing must be stressed: neither the SD Party nor the government ordered local governments to introduce SMCs. What they did was rather like sending a signal: We have an idea here, are you interested? Some respondents spoke about "waves" or "trains" that come: right now it is SMC, "free municipalities," and "municipalities of the future." It is up to the local level to "jump on the bandwagon" or to let it pass. We shall return to the conditions that suggested to some municipalities that they should jump on and to others that they should stay put. But at this stage, it is important to stress this unfocused character of the ideology launching, which was quite different from centrally steered reforms of the 1960s. Nevertheless, there was no doubt about the central support for the ideology:

It is a bit of a question of directives from above, in this case, at least that's how I feel—from the Social Democratic Party. This decentralization policy is really being pushed by the government. The Ministry for Civil Service Affairs has really pushed these matters pretty hard.

And here is a local formulation: a "goal for Submunicipal Committees" as prescribed in one of the local governments studied:

Democracy is a matter of our possibility to decide on the shape of our society. Democracy is not given once and for all. Every generation must achieve it anew. And it is in the municipality where the democratic principles can be best employed. . . . The introduction of Sub-Municipal Committees facilitates contacts between the elected and the electors. What is more, better cooperation between various sectors can increase democracy's potential to unite people in a common effort.

Brunsson (1985) lists a set of conditions that an effective (action-facilitating) ideology must fulfill in order to produce a collective action. It must be conclusive (consist of a limited number of precise normative statements), complex, and consistent. However, every ideology is exposed to an unlimited number of subjective interpretations. Therefore, we can apply only ex post facto reasoning: the fact that an ideology is effective must indicate that there was a sufficient number of people who considered it to be conclusive, complex, and consistent. One can also assume that every interpretation that finds it inconclusive, simplistic, or inconsistent will diminish its effectiveness and will therefore challenge its usefulness as a means of control. There will be many such interpretations quoted in the following analysis. Alternatively, one could ask whether the eventual action was an important goal at all.

The above conditions are of an internal character, relating to the perceived attributes of the ideology. Previous chapters indicated a set of external contingencies that were necessary for the effective use of an ideology. One of the most important was the ideology's links with the cultural context of organizing—more general and older values that are part of the national or international culture, and therefore are widely shared (Chapter 3).

The democracy-via-decentralization ideology was extremely well anchored—in an international myth of Greek democracy and in a Swedish myth of local democracy. Here is an excerpt from a municipal newspaper edited by one of the local governments under study:

"Democracy is a Greek word meaning 'folk rule.' In ancient Greece all free inhabitants . . . met to decide how the state should be governed. . . . " Later, under the headline "Från byalag till kommunfullmäktige" (From village team to local council), the same paper said:

> The people's self-governance in Sweden is a tradition dating from Viking times. The village was the oldest municipal unit. Villagers . . . decided the village law and people used to gather for village assemblies. . . .

And, along these lines, a connection between the Greek tradition, the Swedish tradition, and SMCs was created.

Another important factor, decisive for organizational use of cultural elements, was that such elements have to appeal to important needs or wishes of the people, be they individuals, groups, or societies, to whom the myths, ideologies, rituals are addresed (Chapter 4). The "return to nature" ideology, for instance, had little success in the developing countries. It is not important how "objective" these needs or wishes are. It is important, however, that everyone agrees on their importance.

The major condition for introducing the SMC reform, and the major difference between the municipalities that decided to reform and those that did not, was a factor termed "a strong political will" by the respondents. Translated into ordinary language, it means that all or almost all the important parties wanted the reform. It was not enough that the ruling majority wanted it: if the opposition had not accepted the reform, it would have turned it down at the first opportunity, as cases involving other reforms have shown. Sometimes this political unity may be achieved by blackmailing one of the parties into loyalty to its own party creed, but nevertheless, " . . . it's very important to reach an agreement when you are going to start this sort of activity. Politicians in various parties must be in agreement."

In other words, if an ideology is to be an effective vehicle for change, it must not become an issue for political debate, and it must be seen as answering important needs or wishes, as formulated by the politicians.

Which needs? Which wishes? They could be covert or overt, pertain to long-standing problems or new opportunities. It could be a chance to solve problems arising from the fact that some localities had never accepted the municipal merger, an opportunity for attracting attention (and therefore people and funds), a necessity of conforming to central trends, or a desire to become rebels. When a trainload of ideologies comes from Central Station, municipalities look for something that may fit.

But this is not all. So far, I have spoken about local governments as if they were one-person organizations or, at best, a single group of united politicians. But once a municipality accepts an ideology, it still has to win acceptance within the municipality. Whose acceptance should it be?

When we speak about ideology as a means of and a target for control, it is important to establish who is exercising control and who is subject to control. It is easy to make hasty conclusions about those two matters, especially in light of the actor-intention perspective used in the two previous analyses and, indeed, in most research on control. The intended control dominates the picture. However, the perceptions of the organization's members point toward a different, "situational" picture of control, seen as a result of many conflicting intentions and attempts. The "intentional" definition holds true if actors' attempts at control are by and large successful. This is, however, not always the case.

Therefore, one possible hasty conclusion would be that since politicians decided about "catching" the ideology, it was the politicians who exercised control. But even if politicians unite in a party decision, as individuals they still need to be attracted to a given ideology, just like everybody else. Furthermore, an ideology is a very peculiar means of control: it can be adopted by many and used in unexpected directions. So, for example, a Democracy Committee preparing the reform in one of the municipalities under study was accused by some officers of undemocratic proceedings. I would like to stress that the traditional, unidirectional model of organizational control is in this case too simple to portray organizational happenings. As we shall see now and again, it was often unclear who controlled whom and by what means; and, especially, attempts at control were confused by both actors and observers with the control achieved.

The same reasoning applies to a possible subject of control. One may hastily conclude that it should be citizens, the recipients of local democracy, who are to be subjected to control. But it was not citizens who were to change their way of operating, and it was not citizens' perceptions that were to be the target of change. True, the ideology had to be accepted by the citizens in order to achieve a legitimate status, but they were not subjects for influence. The targets of control were the ideas of members and employees of local governments, and the ideology had to appeal to their needs.

The data showed that this particular ideology was not equally appealing to everybody. It did attract, in the first place, those within the local government who would like to see their professional or political roles as that of standard-bearers of democracy rather than as bureaucrats or political tokens. Second, the ideology appealed to those who had an idealistic, strongly normative picture of the role of the local government as a community benefactor and who perceived reality as defective in this respect. Third, it appealed to those who were reform-minded: any change was, for them, a change for the better. Fourth, the ideology appealed to those who saw it as a chance to gain more autonomy.

How many were attracted, compared with those who were indifferent to the democracy via decentralization ideology? No such measure could be taken or such an estimate made, if only because a belief is not a "yes/no" matter. But, as already stated, ex post facto reasoning can be applied: those who were attracted had to be numerous enough in those municipalities where the ideology fulfilled the controlling role.

Were they numerous or just strong-willed? As the majority usually accepts an organizational status quo and takes it for granted, a person who is willing to accomplish change can go far. It was often the case that people who were steering the municipal merger in the 1960s were now attracted to and involved in a new change.

When we come to the last type of anchorage, the anchorage of an ideology in reality, two meanings of the concept can be evoked in the present context. One is whether an ideology remains purely in the domain of talk, or whether there are some decisions and actions following from it. Within this definition of "reality anchorage," the answer was positive. Even before the ideology was launched full-scale, the Local Bodies' Act gave it solid legal support. Then came the government report, which could be seen both as a planned development of an ideology and as the way to legitimate it. Another meaning denotes the fit between the results of changes brought about by an ideology and the promises the ideology contained (Chapter 2). This fit is the most crucial and the most difficult to assess.

First, there are rarely measures that can show whether an ideology produced a desired change. Has democracy increased as a result of decentralization? There have been no systematic attempts at evaluating the impact of changes on citizens. This could be interpreted as avoidance of an admission of failure, but it could equally well be a commonsense realization that an evaluation is not really possible. A direct survey of opinions concerning the functioning of local governments would have required a sound preexperimental test in order to assess possible changes. And even then, causal reasoning is very risky in such contexts. Indirect indicators, such as the number of active participants in community life, are prone to suffer from even greater dangers of hasty causal reasoning: there are so many other variables (like weather, quality of TV programs, bus and train timetables) that must be controlled. It would take extreme naiveté or ignorance to plunge into such an evaluation. All social events are "overdetermined," Weick (1979) reminds us, and if we can describe some connections that are visible, it would still be too arrogant to claim that we can test the social event we have hypothetically predicted in a satisfactory way.

Second, there is invariably a long delay between the time an ideology is launched and the time the effects become visible. The fact that reforms within the Swedish public sector usually take a very long time is of additional importance here (there is a platitude to support this, that "democracy must take time"). Also, the nonconcrete, symbolic effects fall easy prey to differing interpretations. Reality is always socially interpreted. There are, therefore, good grounds for expecting that the fit between ideology and reality will remain unchallenged until the next ideology emerges.

Third, the optimism of evaluation and efficiency prophets notwithstanding,

. . . what is really difficult to measure is precisely the effect that we are trying to achieve, in terms of service and adaptation of production. How can these things be measured financially? And even worse, how does one measure a sense of belonging and work satisfaction? How can one measure things like that? Participation? Feeling good as a result? The fact that operations improve as a result of increased participation? These sorts of things are difficult to measure.

I am not trying to say that it is impossible to assess a fit between an ideology and reality. As proved by the fate of many ideologies that failed, such assessment is quite realistic, even if it is the interested parties and not the researchers who finally perform it. If an ideology promises better wages and lower prices, then in spite of the possibility of statistical manipulations, reality will sooner or later emerge from beneath the ideology (see Chapter 2). But the less concrete the promised results, and the longer the time allowed, the more difficult it becomes to assess the fit between ideology and reality.

SUPPORTIVE, COMPETITIVE, AND SUBVERSIVE IDEOLOGIES

It is hard to think of an organization that has only one ideology. With the possible exception of some small and fanatical sects, organizations always have room for several ideologies. In total institutions, different ideologies involve different aspects of institutional life (and can be astonishingly incongruent; Kunda 1984). In pluralistic institutions, there are many ideologies, even if one usually clearly dominates.

A supportive ideology is a set of ideas that does not contradict the controlling ideology but supports it with additional, loosely related ideas ("Democracy via decentralization, yes, but also integration"). A competitive ideology is a noncontradictory set of ideas that, however, is perceived by some actors as more important than the dominant ideology ("Democracy via decentralization, maybe, but rather savings!"). It follows that one and the same ideology can be perceived by various actors as either supportive or competitive. A subversive ideology questions the positive value of the leading ideology and suggests alternative hidden negative motives ("Democracy via decentralization indeed; they only meant to accumulate greater power"). It follows that subversive ideologies are always ascribed to others; nobody admits accepting them personally.

It may happen that the same ideology is interpreted as supportive, competitive, or subversive: for example, the "return to old municipalities" ideology. Its supportive interpretation said "It is important to match administrative units with the real communities"; the competitive version said "What we/they really want is to undo the previous reform"; and the subversive version said "It is a local patriotism, and certainly not a need for democracy."

The role of supportive, competitive, and subversive ideologies is, naturally, very important in a situation in which ideology is the main mode of control. Competitive and subversive ideologies are used in countercontrol attempts; and as "talk" becomes a crucial organizational behavior, various ideologies provide it with the contents and arenas for persuasion and dialogue or conflict.

Quite a few ideologies accompanied the leading ideology during the reform.

Integration and Effectiveness

From the beginning integration was one of the main goals of SMC reform. It was understood as an integration of various operations performed in the same geographical area and services provided for the same population. The coordination of the efforts of various specialists, who were often separately involved in dealings with various members of the same family, should lead to an improvement in the quality of results and eventually reduce costs through the avoidance of double expenses. This ideology was clearly supportive. What has been suggested, especially by skeptics, is that this ideology should have been enough, as it is firmly grounded in common sense and experience, as opposed to a much more vague "democracy." Another observation that could make "integration and effectiveness" a candidate for a competitive ideology was that so far the decentralization had been aimed at what was already decentralized: schools and social welfare, offices that had never been centralized. In a situation where both the purpose and the means are unclear, it would perhaps be better to propose something more concrete, some of the respondents argued.

From the point of view of the present analysis, the "integration and effectiveness" ideology does not have enough anchorage to serve as an effective ruling ideology. Common sense and practical experience are good grounds for action, but they are not colorful enough to have a more powerful appeal. There are hardly any myths to which they can be connected. Specialization and professionalization still have much stronger appeal in Western societies than has integration and the holistic approach; competition is seen as more beneficial for organizations than is cooperation; and, as to the vagueness of the final goal, democracy and effectiveness can compete on equal terms.

Efficiency and Savings

There was no agreement on whether "efficiency and savings" was a suppportive or a competitive ideology. According to those who believed it to be supportive, the integration mentioned above should automaticlaly introduce economic gains through a sounder allocation of resources, the avoidance of double functions, and local control. In the eyes of other actors, however, it was a highly subversive ideology:

Then we discussed things the whole time on the basis of a democratic reform, and it was said all the time that this reform is being introduced to give citizens greater influence, and opportunities to decide about their own part of the municipality. But simultaneously, we also have pretty poor finances in this municipality. . . . And then it was said that the reform would mean rationalization and savings. And this does not make sense. If you want to go in for a democratic reform, then it costs money. And that's the sad side of this reform, just now.

The owners of the ruling ideology, the main change agents, rejected the notion that "efficiency and savings" was at any time considered to be a supportive ideology. According to them, the assumption had been that, apart from the necessary reform costs, which should be kept low, no change in operating costs was to be expected. The critics said that such an assumption revealed high optimism in itself, as the costs for reforms are never low. Popular philosophies seemed to be in conflict. According to one philosophy, "Everything that is good must be also expensive"; according to another, "Everything that saves money is good."

Change for Change's Sake

This was clearly a competitive ideology, and a very popular one. According to it, continuous reform is a mark of the Swedish public sector. As it had been more than ten years since the last reform, it was about time to start another. "There are some people who feel well only during a reorganization!" It was suggested that these same people usually headed consecutive reforms.

The main argument of the proponents of this ideology was that "democracy via decentralization" did not seem to be very realistic. There was no direct election to SMCs and why should democracy and local involvement increase as a result of an internal organizational change?

It has been pointed out that the promoters of change had little understanding of organizational dynamics. There are many things that must grow to survive and cannot be mechanically produced. Democracy is one of these. Why should an autocratic reform give birth to increased democracy? This point of view was expressed publicly (*Dagens Nyheter,* April 22, 1985):

Reforms become symbolic actions, something to offer the inhabitants without really changing anything fundamental. . . . Few municipalities dare to say "no!" to something that is in the wind, despite the fact that the evaluations are far from complete. Illusory freedom—more bureaucracy.

According to the proponents of this ideology, the machine ground on, and could be stopped only by the next reform.

Return to Old Municipalities or Undoing the Previous Reform

It has been pointed out that the decentralization attempts had started in those municipalities which had shown most resistance during the merger that took place during the 1970s. Indeed, it is easy to imagine, for example, that old towns with long traditions would fight against their incorporation into another unit and would welcome a return to old administrative divisions.

In a supportive version of this ideology, it has been stressed that the work of an SMC should be based on the community feelings among people living within a geosocial district. This operation, however, attracted a strong suspicion that a subversive ideology, aiming at undoing the merger, was at work. Therefore, alternative solutions were considered: cake-slice division of the territory, borders following water, and mixed solutions were all employed to counteract such a perception.

The subversive version of the ideology was still very strong:

The Center Party follows this line, because they want to go back to the old division of municipalities that we had before 1971. They think that we ought to have direct elections in the SMC, and ultimately they would like to break up these large municipalities into small municipalities once more.

If the presence of this ideology was clearly noted, the opinions on it differed. Many respondents interpreted it as an irrational nostalgia and parochialism:

Many people like to produce memories of how it was in the old municipality, they are happy to romanticize, but the truth is that it was messy. There was no money to do anything. But they do not remember that—they remember that it was idyllic, and that's how they would like to have it again. Because then, there was something to argue about, at any case. Now, they could not care less what you think, those bureaucrats, say the romantics. But we do not live under those circumstances any more!

As this subversive ideology was very strong, and therefore danger-ous, it was counteracted by yet another version of the "return to old municipalities" ideology, which might be seen as competitive but not subversive: a "repairing" ideology:

Many people thought [during the merger] that now we are building up a big municipality, now we shall really have resources, but they forgot the democ-racy aspect—people's opportunities to participate actively in decisions and to acquire good insight and information about the working of the municipality. We often talk about the distance between the decision makers, the bureaucrats, the politicians, and the citizens—the distance between them increased, and we didn't get too many years into the 1970s before people realized that this must be repaired and corrected in some way, but they were not prepared to go back to the old municipal divisions. They tried to find new ways that people could try to maintain the collective municipal resources in an area, but make im-provements to increase and reinforce influence. This is what we call municipal democracy.

Power Shift

Clearly supportive and widely noticed, if never officially formu-lated, this ideology suggests that the need for reform was born from a dissatisfaction concerning the allocation of control possibilities. The growing size and complexity of organizations caused a reduction in political control and an increase in administrative control. Politicians found themselves lost in a jungle of information they could not pro-cess.

A suspicion grew that this complexity was exploited by central of-ficers, who were highly competent professionals, to take the steering wheel. An unintentional and diffused coup d'état.

So a possible main goal of the reform was to change matters: to give politicians a better opportunity to steer. This ideology was perceived as neither competitive nor subversive: "Politicians are representatives of the people. Giving more power to them is giving more power to the people." In practice, it meant a strengthening of the Municipal Executive Committee, quite possibly with an accompanying growth of the importance of the central offices that serve it directly, at the expense of specialized committees and specialized offices.

Political Development

According to this ideology, the present reform was just a further step in the search for increased democracy, which was initiated with the SMC experiment, continued in the idea of social welfare districts, and finally resulted in the SMC reform. This ideology was actually a variant of the ruling ideology, only it placed the latter in a row of similar approaches and not as *the* ideology.

It was seen as a competitive ideology by the representatives of the parties who had proposed previous solutions and by officers who had taken part in earlier experiments. "Nothing new under the sun" was the underlying tone of this interpretation of the reform.

Along the same lines, it was also pointed out that the present reform was legally possible thanks to the Local Bodies' Law, passed by the bourgeois government. The reform was therefore just a logical conclusion of previous developments.

Political Expediency

Another competitive ideology was that the decentralization was simply to create new political posts, and therefore would activate internal party life rather that the local community. Recruitment and active involvement had become serious problems:

If you look at the political side, it's an aged organization. We are suffering from a "sclerosis" in the worst sense of the word in the political parties, and you can't really hope to convince young girls to take part in it. They were, for a very short time, but now they do not want to work with us. It's the "heavy boys" who stay on. . . .

Which party was mainly interested? The idea had been born elsewhere, but life was breathed into it under the Social Democrat rule.

This came as a surprise, as, according to a common opinion, expressed here by one of the respondents:

. . . in the Social Democratic Party, in the 1970s, people have not been particularly interested in such extensive decentralization, setting up submunicipal councils and committees. These were the lines the Center Party and the liberals have followed . . . but then there was a certain swing at the end of the 1970s, and the Social Democratic side pushed very hard to renew political life. The Social Democrats did a turnaround, not only here, in this municipality, but in the country as a whole. There was this lack of political interest, lack of new political recruits, and difficulties in recruiting young people and getting political involvement at a grass-roots level.

It was pointed out that the Social Democratic Party is well known (and both criticized and admired) for its ability to "catch" promising ideas, regardless of the source. "Local democracy" is one example; "market elements," another: both were originally launched by the bourgeois government but put to efficient use by the Social Democrats.

However, the other parties had similar recruitment problems, and therefore considered it expedient to join forces. Or, at least, speculated that it would be.

What is interesting in this ideology is its metacharacter. Its contents are actually an interpretation of another ideology, the ruling one.

Anarchistic Ideology

One of the "smaller" ideologies was the anarchistic approach (the "organic order"). It was a supportive ideology that claimed the state of decentralization is closer to the state of organic order, where grass-roots control dominates and no unnecessary bureaucratic overheads are maintained. It was, indeed, close to the idea of the most conventional anarchistic movements, such as neighborhood self-government movements in the United States. Some of the reform's ideologues took inspiration from the thought of Spanish and Swedish anarchists.

This ideology was, however, used in moderation and too much visible anchorage was avoided: for the majority of people anarchism still means bomb-throwing and chaos. But for a certain elite, anarchy's "organic order" might be more attractive than social democracy. The

problem is, of course, whether it is possible to have an anarchy introduced by institutions.

An (Almost) Missing Ideology: Organizational Development

An organization theorist cannot help but notice that such splendid
reasons for decentralizing such as the size of organizations and their
resulting complexity were scarcely mentioned. A company that employs 4,000 people is called an "industrial empire," but a local government that employs 5000 people is a "small" one. SKF, a well-
known roller-bearing producer located in Gothenburg, employs fewer
people than does the West District office in the recreation administration in Gothenburg's local government. Volvo Corporation employs
about 75,000 people worldwide, more than are in Gothenburg's local
government (65,000), but less than are in the local government if only
Swedish-based companies are counted.

We could not but poke around in the hope that somebody would be
convinced that it was high time for local governments to decentralize
in order to optimize their organizational functions. The answer was
negative: No, the opposite, if anything. But we received a confirmation of the observation that local governments have a "miniaturizing"
self-image. The explanation was that this self-image was built as a
reflection of the public image:

> Society at large does not know, for example, that the highways office is larger
> than a major company, which has as many employees as we have, and that
> our activities are so manifold. Most people think that the director of the high-
> ways office is out there shoveling snow, and what the others do, that's a real
> question. . . .

But ultimately, even if the public image of local government is dis-
torted, there are municipalities and local governments that are un-
doubtedly very large organizations. Ought they not to decentralize first?
"I believe that the smaller the municipality, the better the chance for
SMCs," said a respondent from one of the "small" governments.
Why?

In a larger municipality, there would be such a helluva mass of submunicipal committees that it would be hard to find any sense in the whole thing. It would be just a big mess.

A respondent from a large municipality agrees wholeheartedly:

Submunicipal committees are most appropriate in medium-size and in small municipalities. It's very difficult to introduce the submunicipality concept into a large municipality. We have so many activities that are rather specific in a large municipality and can't be split among various local committees. There is a pretty big pile of joint and mutual municipal cooperations. . . .

A conclusion that the reform best suited small and middle-size municipalities was very popular, although the underlying reasoning could vary greatly. Apart from the above quotation, we have encountered the argument that all large entreprises require concentrated resources and that it has nothing to do with size as such but with a degree of previous centralization: only governments that were previously highly centralized can expect positive results from decentralization.

However, very few respondents excluded the possibility that all large municipalities would, in time, introduce SMCs if there was a political will to do so. The resistance, or rather the delay is taking a decision, in big cities was often explained by the fact that their political weight gave them more discretion in acceptance of the proposed ideology than was the case for small municipalities.

STRUCTURE

The leading ideology described the reform as a decentralization, a change in the structure of control. Following the intentions of the change promoters, as reflected in formal decisions and supporting documents, a new desired structure of that part of local government which was included in the reform could be reconstructed as shown in Figure 5.1.

According to this plan, citizens control the municipal and submunicipal commissioners by political means, and, as clients, they can also try to influence local officers and submunicipal coordinators (who represent the leading group in the figure). A municipal council can influence submunicipal commissioners and members of specialized committees via party channels and, via its executive committee, the central

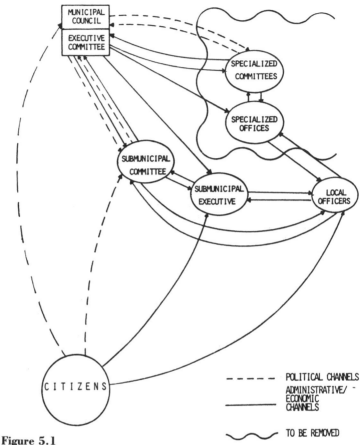

Figure 5.1
Control Processes in a Decentralized Local Government

municipal administration and submunicipal coordinators. Specialized committees control appropriate parts of the central municipal administration, which in turn control local officers within a given specialty.

The broken lines in the figure symbolize control through purely political channels, whereas solid lines indicate control transmitted by administrative/economic channels. At least theoretically, most of these relationships should be reciprocal.

It is possible that the above plan will become a reality, but in the meantime the process of reform introduced a new structure. The fact that control was ideological contributed to the fact that this structure can hardly be presented in the form of a traditional organizational design. Nevertheless, quite new positions have been created, and an interesting set of relationships was built among them. A tentative picture is presented in figure 5.2.

The lines joining the positions indicate what kind of organizational behavior (talk or action) is used to control (or to countercontrol, to oppose) another position.

Choosing the names for positions, I decided to mix metaphors. I do not want to say that local governments are like political parties or like churches: I would like to show that local governments have elements in common with organizations that, by design, use ideological control as a dominant mode.

Our respondents used most of the metaphors themselves. They were also of mixed, political-religious character: they spoke about "bishops," "ideologues," "conservatives" and "progressives," "religious messages," and the like.

Ideology Owners

It was perhaps most difficult to characterize the ideology owners. Their two most obvious traits were their clear subscription to the ideology and their role of change agents. They could be, however, both politicians and officers, and the most unclear issue was how they became the "owners" of the ideology. They were rarely the inventors, or at least did not present themselves as such. Sometimes they indicated the origins of the ideology within their party; sometimes they pointed to the outside, to free research and the intellectual world.

If one had to be precise in delineating this group, a relevant grouping would then be the members of the reform committee (which has had different names in different municipalities). If a broader and less specific grouping principle is sought, then it would be politicians rather than officers, and Social Democrats rather than other parties. This search led to the discovery of an interesting subgroup, nominal ideology owners. Usually central-level politicians and Social Democrats, they loyally followed the party line and fulfilled the main task of ideology owners: to spread the ideology ("I am one of them when I am there, outside, at a party meeting, and we speak much about it, and they are very positive about it"). But, if they were, for example, members of

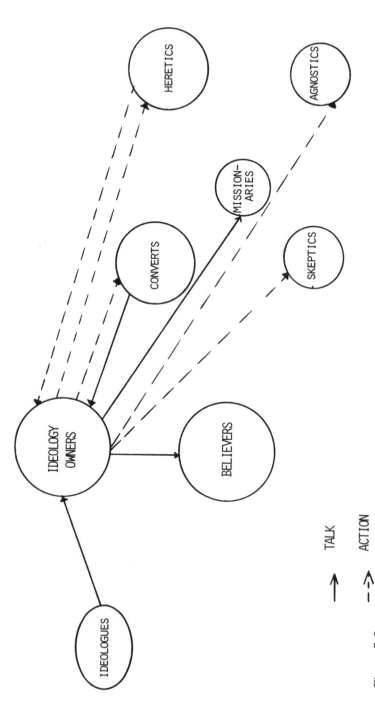

Figure 5.2
Ideological Control Structure

specialized committees, they were perceived as opposing the reform by action in accordance with the old rules. One could have the impression that they would gladly join the heretics, but that was not the role allocated to them. (As we shall see, role casting was an important phenomenon within ideological control.)

One of the original ideas in finding a name for the ideology owners' group was "ideology users." But then it appeared that this was not a specific group. Practically everybody (but heretics) could use ideology in attempts at control: local officers, to remind central officers of the new rules of the game; local politicians, in trying to encourage professionals to cooperate; central officers, to show central politicians that they sinned against what they preached. This was one of the most interesting traits of ideological control: that, unless cast as an ideological enemy, anybody could adopt the ideology and try to use it.

Ideologues

Ideologues were employed by the ideology owners in order to formulate and reformulate ideology, to decorate and embellish it, and to help propagate it. They were actually a marketing department, but more within than outside the organization: they took care of the product and its marketing.

This analogy is, however, of limited use: in the course of the presentation, it will become clear, now and again, how different they were from the ideologues found in the private sector.

Let us start from the top. There was an ideologue employed centrally:

. . . the "light knight from Härnösand," as he is sometimes called, the minister of civil affairs, who is sort of an ideologue in this area, and who says that all kinds of decentralization have only good sides.

He had his equivalents at the local level. If the usefulness of their role was fully appreciated, there were also some complaints about the ideologues' distance from reality:

He is more of a visionary, like Jesus in these questions, and we all agreed that it's necessary. He plays an important role—in that he has very good political connections centrally, as I see it. And he is an excellent visionary.

He collects information from other people, he will willingly spread information to others, but he is not as well anchored in the submunicipal committees that we have here. And it's probably for that reason that our people don't meet him so much anymore, we do not have the energy to deal with all the clippings and books and newspapers and all that sort of thing.

And that was, I thought, the main difference between ideologues from the public and the private sectors. In the latter, ideologues are either managers or consultants. Both are very practically oriented. For the ideologues of the SMC reform, the reform had mainly the character of an intellectual experiment rather than of a structural reorganization. Respondents frequently said; "It is not so much a question of changing structures as of changing attitudes."

It follows, then, that the ideologues' picture of the reform and the representation of the ideology were complex, tinged with doubts and a far cry from simplistic snapshots produced by typical propaganda officers. As one of them said:

Sometimes I am surprised by my own attitude to these questions. There has been opposition to this and there still is. Some doubt: It costs money. And it's getting more and more expensive. It will be more bureaucratic. It does not promote progress. It is better to have this sort of central expertise that we have today. People do not understand it. People do not care about it. But, for my part, even if I think about all this, I believe in this, unconditionally. It hasn't changed in any way.

There were other versions, too: a more pragmatic, flexible, and easy-to-contact joker trying to keep the ideology on the ground by letting the pomposity out of it; a researcher introducing the status of his discipline. Most likely the type of ideologue who was employed depended on the available options. If I focused my attention on the first type, it was because of its originality. Organizations do not very often employ dreamers, and it is perhaps the public sector's privilege to be able to do so.

Prophets were a special type of ideologue—retired top politicians, researchers, or philosophers—who had supposedly dealt with the issues central to reform a long time ago. The reference to "prophets" gave the ideology a historically more stable, more rooted character, rather similar to its anchorage in myths.

Believers

The believers could be found mostly among local politicians, but also among local officers. What distinguished them from the ideology owners was that they neither knew nor seemed to be interested in the total ideology. They took the parts of the ideology that were of use to them and interpreted it in a pragmatic manner. This is probably a trait common to all believers. Their cut-down-to-real-size ideologies may seem sacrilegious to some ardent ideologues or ideology owners, but they work in practice.

Brunsson (1985) tells us that, in order to facilitate action, ideologies must be concrete. Our observations permit a broadening of this insight. It seems that a successful ideology must, in fact, be vague enough to permit many individuals to connect with it. At the same time, it must be concrete enough to be identified as the same ideology in which they all believe. One more trait of the believers was that they showed the strongest reaction against the heretics, who were usually central officers.

Heretics

Heretics were perhaps the most interesting group within the structure. They did not become heretics by choice: they were cast as such by the ideology owners.

It was often said that the professionalization of certain services was the most serious obstacle in the decentralization experiments (Jönsson 1985). People who belong to highly developed professional structures, for example, the school system, do not want to cross the boundaries of their professional system in order to establish contact with people outside of the system, expecially not with nonprofessionals. The cohesion of a professional system is postulated to be greater than that of an organizational system (Scott 1985).

I would like to point out that, as with most of organizational processes, the phenomenon is two-directional. The heretics in the reform studied were appointed from among the professional officers. They were supposed to oppose the reform. One begins to suspect that a self-fulfilling prophecy might have had some role in the process.

Many of them accepted the role. Sometimes this acceptance was accompanied by a sense of bewilderment, as in the case of a new officer employed by the central administration with the apparent purpose of helping the experiment (the old executive would probably have opposed the reform very seriously, and not only as a matter of a role playing). However, the officer very soon discovered that he had been cast as a heretic. After some time he became used to the new role and accepted it.

A typical heretic produced subversive ideologies and, generally, challenged the ideological bluff:

It's a pseudo democracy. There has been an attempt to make the people believe that democracy would be increased by expanding the number of committees. The only thing you gain with this is that you get certain people more interested in politics, but it's only people who sit on the committees. You don't increase the interest of the, so to speak, common man.

An interesting situation was created if persons who were cast as heretics because of their formal position aspired to join the ideology owners. The confusion was far-reaching. Ideology owners treated such cases with suspicion. Nevertheless, such a situation was most stressful for heretics themselves: "It is a thankless task, as I see it, that whatever you do is wrong. Either central politicians see it like that, or local politicians."

It is important to note that what was most visible in the case of heretics was probably true of all the roles: that the way they were cast was dictated by their organizational position not by their personal attitudes.

Converts

Some of the "previously appointed" heretics were given a chance to convert. This happened in situations where the formal position of a person automatically qualified him/her as a heretic, and yet his/her cooperation was necessary for the implementation of planned change. They faced a clear-cut alternative: to quit or to convert. A third, theoretical possibility—that of taking part in a process that one personally opposes—must be seen as too demanding to be given serious consideration.

There were, basically, two mechanisms for conversion. One was the social norm, the old definition of an officer as a loyal public servant who is to serve but not necessarily to agree:

. . . my position, as responsible to the executive committee, makes it essential that I fulfill their political decisions. So that when the executive committee said that my office, which is the organization for executing changes, should take on this job, the time for trial and error was over. . . . And this is a question of either-or; if you can't do it, you might as well forget it!

The other mechanism of conversion was attitude change, facilitated by special courses. These courses, in overcoming resistance to change or in leadership, aimed at increased awareness of sources of resistance and a deepened insight. So, with an underlying change of attitude or out of loyalty to the public service, potential heretics were allowed to escape their original role and join the ideology owners or the believers—by becoming converts.

Skeptics

Skeptics were those who believed in the idea of democracy and the need for it at the local level, but experienced problems in noting the connection between present developments and the main idea. In other words, they saw the ideology as inconsistent. Usually they saw the organizational change as quite useful, but they viewed the "blowing-up" action skeptically and refused the ideological approach. Sometimes they were irritated with the excessively ardent believers, and refused to get carried away on the wings of almost religious feelings.

Some people take the view that out in the field everything will take care of itself, but I think this is due to some form of thinking which almost resembles religion. They have no ties with reality. There are certain people . . . you can't talk SMCs with, who don't see any problems with decentralization. They only see advantages, and I think it's a defect when you are so single-minded and shortsighted.

Agnostics

Agnostics did not feel that it was necessary to introduce ideological elements into the explanation of current events. From their point of view, a decision for organizational change had been made from above, and it was clear that individual or local resistance was not going to alter it. Therefore one had to follow along, adopt what seemed sensible, and beware of absurdities or redundancies.

This is something that is going to come, and that you can't just be negative about. Then you would just go under. This is something that we are going to live with, and you have to have a positive approach to it, but then you also have to point out to the politicians, on every occasion, what is it they really want?

Agnostics were perhaps the most difficult target to tackle: the efforts of ideology owners and ideologues were lost on them, by definition. They were immune to the dominant mode of control. But they often perceived the reform as being a chance to realize some objectives that had nothing to do with the leading ideology. And therefore they co-operated, even if their purposes might contradict the official goal of the reform.

Missionaries

Missionaries were the believers who adopted the ideology most fully and then were sent out of the world of ideas into the real world to spread the gospel.

Unfortunately, life among skeptics, agnostics, and heretics proved to be very frustrating for the missionaries. The ideology owners turned out to be not much help. The problem of the missionaries was that they did not know about the gap between the two worlds—the world of talk and the world of action—and some of them got lost in the abyss. Their doubts increased, or were kept bottled up and were revealed only through the safety valve of another role.

. . . one is inclined to believe that one has been pushed by the parties, when one might prefer more pushing from the people. If I take myself as an individual and an inhabitant of the municipality, then I know that there are an enormous number of people who discuss municipal questions at dinners and in their spare time, who are not politically involved and who don't know how to influence things. . . .

Sometimes, though, the pressure became too strong, and missionaries felt betrayed and alone with their faith in the ideology. The criticism, however, was never open and was usually disguised in personal expressions of faith:

What I feel has been the most important for *me,* which *I* wanted to work for all the time, is the goals and objectives concerning inhabitants, expansion of democracy—so that people who lived in my area would have very clear, direct contact routes, and that it should be possible to influence things.

There were two strategies for surviving in this difficult situation. One was "mixing with the natives," but only to a certain degree: without the necessity of divorcing oneself from the ideology owners. This attitude encompassed a multiple perspective: "I still believe in the ideology, but I am not blind to its costs."

The other strategy was a distancing strategy: giving up the exposed missionary's position and moving to another, in order not to lose the faith altogether.

PROCESSES AFFECTED BY IDEOLOGICAL CONTROL

Talk

I have talked much, as I usually do. But then, I am a politician.

It was mentioned in the preceding section that the bearers of various positions used different behaviors in order to promote or to oppose the reform. Documents, speeches, information leaflets, and special courses were employed to transmit and establish the ideology. However, talk was a weak instrument when applied to heretics. Here, the main instrument of control became action in the form of a decision. Ideology owners rarely involved themselves in any more concrete action, and this fact was often pointed out by the heretics, skeptics, and agnostics. Indeed, decisions were more closely coupled to talk than to action: they were often wordy, and it was hard to deduce what specific action should have stemmed from them.

Having noted these discrepancies, we turn back to the observation that talk is a "natural" means of achieving ideological control. This is done through such obvious means as documents and speeches. I would like to focus on less noticeable, and therefore more interesting, uses of talk that were mentioned in Chapter 3: the labeling process, the use of platitudes, and the purposes of metaphors.

The most important label was "decentralization." Calling something "decentralization" in the 1980s is as positive as labeling something "centralization" had been in the 1960s. Decentralization is, by definition, good. However, as many studies point out (see DiTomaso 1985), almost identical organizational or political changes may be called "centralization" or "decentralization," depending on the intentions of label producers and on current fashion. Even more positivist, classic decentralization studies (such as Blau 1970) note the relativity of the concepts of centralization and decentralization, and try to resolve the issue in a way that can be best summarized with the help of one of the platitudes used in the SMC reform: "Every decentralization requires some centralization."

Weick (1985; see also Chapter 3) tells us that labels help to control by removing ambiguity. Labels differ, however, in the degree of their concreteness, and therefore in the degree of ambiguity they are able to remove. Compare "this is a cost" and "that is a decentralization." We know that the former is bad and the latter is good, but the detail of diagnosis and specificity of indicated action differ. Costs must be reduced, but decentralization can only be introduced, and there are many ways of achieving it. Broad, abstract labels of that kind are very useful as a control device, because they permit a flexible redefinition of steps to be taken. "This is a cost" defines the value ("costs are bad") and limits the scope of action (there are not many means of cost reduction). "This is a decentralization" defines the value ("decentralizations are good") but opens a great vista of possibilities ("we may even have to centralize in order to decentralize.")

As to the platitudes, it has been said that their main function in organizational settings is to remove uncertainty. It is therefore reasonable to expect many platitudes in a situation of organizational change, which by definition is filled with uncertainty. Indeed, there was a whole set of platitudes that seemed to be an inherent part of the reform. Here is a partial list:

Democracy is not given once and for all.
Democracy has to take its time.

We have created a living municipal democracy.

Every decentralization requires a corresponding centralization (and vice versa).

You have to break down the sector borderlines.

We have to counteract "territory-thinking."

One has to increase the opportunities for people to come nearer to the decisions (and vice versa).

We ought to go out to people with this activity.

There are to be short lines between execution and decision.

You make a shorter line between the idea and the action.

Decision makers must anchor themselves better in reality.

Central units must retain overall responsibility.

Some respondents laughed after having uttered these sentences, in order to distance themselves from the platitude as a rhetorical tool. However, they nonetheless used the platitudes, I believe, for precisely the reason that has been mentioned: to relate to a certain shared value, observation, or way of thinking, and to indicate to us to which school of thought they belonged.

This use of platitudes and other verbal rituals was earlier observed by students of ideological organizations:

In politics, as in religion, whatever is ceremonial or banal strengthens reassuring beliefs regardless of their validity and discourages skeptical inquiry about disturbing issues. (Edelman 1977, p. 3)

The use of metaphors is, in a sense, opposite and complementary to the use of platitudes. Here are some examples:

It's a little like lifting yourself up by your bootstraps. (The accompanying poster showed the local government lifting itself by its bootstraps.)

Coordinators must be primus inter pares.

Central administrative offices are becoming an elephants' graveyard.

It's a way of breathing new life into the dead party organizations.

We got this rich flora of experiments (or flora of reports).

The integration of the social welfare administration has produced a fantastic mastodon.

"Rich flora of experiments" is perhaps the best example of a well-coined metaphor. It projects an image of something blooming, colorful, spontaneous, but also uncontrolled, hard to walk across. Various respondents accentuated different aspects of the metaphor. "To blow life into dead organizations" is not far from the platitude "We have made a living democracy," and reminds us that successful metaphors, after being used for a long time, become platitudes. The first person who said "eyes like stars" was the author of one of the most successful metaphors ever, but by now it has become one of the oldest platitudes.

And, finally, a metaphor that failed. "Primus inter pares" (the first among equals) was meant to denote the coordinator's role in the "collective leader team" but failed miserably, as everybody within the team felt threatened.

Coping with Resistance to Change

Talk and action are formal categories of organizational behavior. If we are interested in the substance, we must look for behaviors that are change-specific. Is a change controlled by ideology any different from other organizational changes? A review of problems related to the division of labor and the building of new roles (Czarniawska-Joerges 1986) shows that, from the point of view of organizational change, the SMC reform could be seen as an extremely skillful or an extremely clumsy way of introducing change. The ambiguousness of social representations characterizing this case haunted me throughout the study. So, here again, I shall present both praise and criticism, starting with a normative picture conveyed by the respondents and ending with an attempt to relate the manner in which change was introduced into the ruling ideology.

It appeared that reform is a norm. Changes occur all the time, but unlike "continuous change" (Beksiak et al. 1978), they have the character of a single, broad reform; unlike discrete changes, they happen repeatedly and within small time intervals. The result is a system in which reform is one of the most common traits. However, it is closer to the discretely changing systems in that the changes are introduced from above, and not from below.

One could therefore interpret reform as contradicting the ruling ideology, where democracy is the main concept. That would be an incorrect conclusion: according to the logic of the ideology, change is a proof of democracy.

This specific understanding of democracy (in terms of openness to the voice of the people, as expressed via party organizations; for the ideal of democracy, see Himmelstrand 1960) and of organizational development (as change introduced by political leaders) must be kept in mind, as it constitutes the key to understanding the whole reform. For example, the opinion "When you make changes in an organization, you have to make them on the basis of demands and needs out here" should be understood as involving not shop-floor employees but "people" as represented by political organizations. One of our respondents made an interesting slip that represented the situation very well. He divided the population of the municipality into "people, politicians, and employees." Democracy for some of those does not have to be the democracy for others.

There was a fund of knowledge of the conditions for successful change, accumulated, one might believe, in the course of many years of experience. First, a reform must take a very long time. Partly this is because the administration is very resistant. No wonder reforms follow each other so closely.

A municipal administration reacts to control sluggishly, and it takes time to put through changes. So when you've carried out that change, then it's time for the next one.

Second, in this specific reform, whose ultimate purpose is a change in political activity at the local level, the waiting time is even longer:

We mustn't make the mistake of going out and thinking that you can achieve any results over one or two electoral periods, because this is a long process. That comes as a surprise, if you've been to some of these seminars, when you hear professors discuss this matter as if they believed that it was possible to change things in a couple of years. That really astonishes you.

Third, people are naturally prone to oppose a change, at least in the beginning. This places a new demand on time: people have to "live in their new roles. . . . For many, it takes a couple of years—to perceive the change, to oppose it, then to reassess their own thinking and to begin to work in a new way."

Finally, one could foresee that the initial lack of role clarity and related uncertainty can lead to conflicts. These should be avoided, in accordance with the cultural norm:

It's obvious that conflicts can occur anywhere in municipal operations. And it happens from time to time. And then you have to do what we do in such cases in Sweden. You have to compromise a little.

What was the prescription for successful reform?

Get hold of an outside project manager who . . . has some local links. Keep him out of the normal change apparatus. Start up an experimental operation. Then, as time goes by, slip him and his ideas into the administration. Get them to support him.

The idea is that when we establish submunicipal committees, that they have rather vague objectives and we have considerable freedom. On the one hand, they have to teach themselves, and on the other hand, the central level has to learn, too, and then things develop. It's not a change in the administration, but a change in an approach.

As we can see, it was also a prescription for an ideologically controlled reform. Did the prescription work?

In the first place, even the most patient ideology owners had to admit that the time span was longer than any of them ever believed. One of the main reasons, as seen by many respondents, was that the ideology owners were much too idealistic in their predictions and had neglected the human factor in their expectations. The lesson learned by those who went far with the experiment was that personnel management has demands that may be in conflict with an ideological reform.

The extreme duration of the experimentation period created uncertainty among many of the people involved, and the continuity of this experience contributed to a fatigue and disenchantment with the ideology as such:

We can sort of settle down again . . . it's probably this uncertainty and all the visions in between that have made us tired. It creates a hiatus that can be filled by speculations, pondering, and various aspects and feelings that draw on your energy. You don't have time for the other things. It's not easy. This can take a hell of a time. And it's not so simple.

Nevertheless, the conclusions formulated by the ideology owners were optimistic. The following excerpt from a municipal document summarizing the experiment restates the relationship between the method of introducing change and the ruling ideology, summarizes how resistance was dealt with, and finally declares the reform a success:

"Learning strategy" is a *democratic* form of change. . . . Ultimately, perhaps there are a few people who never become adjusted to the objectives and purposes of the reform. But in this context it should be pointed out that the reform is now moving into an implementation phase in which it is no longer meaningful for the administration to question the reform's existence. The experiment has primarily been a question of changing attitudes, not of finding finite, definitive organizational solutions. The proposal is a milestone in the history of our municipality. We will achieve a decentralized "large" municipality.

A pragmatic commentator added: "If we are wrong, we are going to have another reorganization, whenever that becomes necessary. We will know when we see it."

REFORMS, IDEOLOGIES, AND PUBLIC SECTORS

The wind of change is blowing strongly through the municipalities of the country.

The preceding section can be the basis for two observations: first, that there were certain characteristics that should have hindered the reform but did not, and second, that the processes created by the change did not seem exactly new or reform-specific. The latter observation seems to provide a good explanation for the former.

All through the structure, there was a strong optimism concerning the fate of the reform. There were equally strong doubts about its effects, but none about its fate: the SMCs were to become a reality. Was this not a little surprising in light of the fact that nobody seemed to agree on anything and that organizational democracy was clearly being sacrificed for political democracy? And yet, if Murphy's Law says "If anything can go wrong, it will," the Swedish law of decentralization seemed to be "If anything can go well, it will."

The most prevalent impression was that most of the actors were very accustomed to the state of reform and to the way it was accomplished: to ideological control as a dominant mode. Some actors claimed, though, that it was a new phenomenon, as previous reforms were based on more traditional types of organizational control. Some others pointed out that there were always "leading" ideologies, and the present ideology was just the most recent version. There was also an explanation of the role of ideology as the rationalization of change that was the result of necessity, the excessive size of long expanding organizations. In light of this explanation, the "missing ideology" (decentralization forced by size) was missing precisely because it was not an ideology but a realistic description of the situation: "It's always better to have some kind of legitimating general ideology than to recognize that one operates on the basis of some sort of realized necessity."

How are ideologies chosen or created? Partly this depends on the external situation, on societal developments:

. . . in every age reform has its reason and its special conditions. In the postwar period, we have experienced an enormous transformation of Swedish society. There was a whole line of such factors as demographic shifts and such like that made these municipal mergers "necessary," so that you have to have larger units, you have to have viable companies that can acquire resources. And then the process has gone on and the population has become better educated, and makes quite new demands—to be able to influence things. We've had the development of the mass media, which means that awareness of what is happening in society is increasing. Take all these questions of environmental discussion, for example. These opinions must be caught up in the political system in some way, if we are not to land up in . . . we have seen where it can lead!

Apart from changes in societal consciousness, there are changes in economic conditions. As suggested before, prosperous times tend to produce material "offerings" from the public sector to its clients, whereas austerity swings the pendulum to more "spiritual" offerings, such as democracy.

It can also be said that every new reform, like every new technology, solves certain problems and creates others; hence the need for the next reform or the next technology, and certainly for a new ideology.

How "Swedish" are these phenomena? To what degree are they culture-bound and to what degree are they universal?

. . . more or less continual, but piecemeal, changes in administrative structures and procedures have been supplemented periodically by more grandiose,
and more explicit, efforts to review and reorganize the administrative apparatus of government. These comprehensive reviews of administrative structure
and practices have been undertaken by governments of all political persuasions
and under a wide variety of political circumstances. They have often involved
considerable investment of money, time and political discussion. They are a
characteristic feature of twentieth-century bureaucratic and political life. (March
and Olsen 1983, p. 281)

So reforming *is* a typical governmental activity. Indeed, it can be
seen in various countries, and in both central and local governments.

Italy

The city council of Bologna introduced neighborhood councils in
1962. The idea quickly spread, and when an appropriate law was passed
in 1976, 60 percent of the cities had already introduced the change
(Dente and Regonini 1980). The Italian case is perhaps closest to the
Swedish, and not by accident: the Italian example was taken into consideration while the Swedish reform was being prepared (Amnå et al.
1985).

The same ideology ("democracy via decentralization") was used
and, similarly, it operated mostly within the domain of talk:

Municipal decentralization philosophy was always linked with an emphasis on
popular participation, either to create "schools of democracy" . . . or to
mobilize new groups so as to change the power realities underlying the administrative system to the advantage of underprivileged groups. . . . Apart
from this general purpose, often declared in official statements but seldom
pursued in practice, the day-to-day tasks of the councils were mainly advisory
at the discretion of the municipalities. (Dente and Regonini 1980, p. 192)

However, the ideology did not serve as a dominant mode of control,
but solely as a means of legitimation. It so happened that the economic
crisis came upon Italian municipalities right in the middle of ideological control.

In 1975 nearly all the largest Italian cities changed their political majorities
and went left. . . . The traditional leftist policy in municipalities (as for in-

stance in Bologna over a long period of time) has been to increase the quantity and quality of public services stimulating at the same time citizen involvement in local politics. The financial crisis, however, made any consistent increase in public services impossible and often caused a reduction of them. (Dente and Regonini 1980, pp. 194-195)

Therefore it was action (behavioral) control that became a dominant mode of control in Italian municipalities under reform. Laws at the central/state level and regulations at the local/municipal level were the main means of control. Experimental, carefully detailed budget procedures were the most important part of the reform.

The United States at the Turn of the Century

Another case is interesting because of its dramatic difference in space and time. Tolbert and Zucker (1983) analyzed the diffusion of civil service reform in the years 1880-1935 in the United States. The reform they analyze can be seen as being composed of two trends: a hierarchically controlled reform (I would call it "action controlled") and an ideologically controlled reform. In some states (New York, Massachusetts, and Ohio) the reform was obligatory. In others it was not, yet many city governments adopted the reform anyway. This voluntary adoption can be seen as being ruled by an ideology of rationalization. It is easy to see the analogy between this reform and the Swedish municipal merger (1970s), on the one hand, and the SMCs, on the other. Unfortunately, the differences between hierarchically and ideologically controlled reform on which this study focuses are mechanical: under the former, the pace of adoption was much faster than under the latter.

There are, however, some interesting similarities between the voluntary adoption and the SMC reform. Thus, the leading ideology of rationalization had to fight competitive and subversive ideologies:

While civil service reform was promoted by the Progressive Movement as increasing the efficiency and effectiveness of the administration of local government, some historians have argued that civil service reform was used as a political weapon by social groups . . . to gain or to maintain their political dominance. (Tolbert and Zucker 1983, p. 30)

What arouses some doubt is whether the main focus of interest for the authors—what makes the difference between early and late adopters—holds true for an ideologically controlled reform:

Therefore, to the extent that an organization is an early adopter of an innovation in formal structure, its decision to adopt will depend on the degree to which the change improves internal processes (for example, by streamlining procedures of reducing conflict).

In contrast, once historical continuity has established their importance, changes in formal structure are adopted because of their societal legitimacy, regardless of their value for the internal functioning of the organization. (Tolbert and Zucker 1983, p. 26)

There are indications pointing in the same direction in our study: the municipalities that were first had specific problems: one wanted to attract attention and enliven its municipal life, others had problems with the old municipalities. Later, it was more a matter of "keeping up." But it is more likely that even late adopters hope that some internal problems can be solved by the reform (as can be clearly seen in the case of the Swedish public sector following the reforms of the private sector, with a delay but precisely in the hope of solving its problems), and that the early adopters also care for legitimacy. If a given reform has not yet acquired the whole glory of legitimacy, we might still argue that reforms as such are legitimating devices within the public sector, and therefore it is a matter of deciding *which* reform has the best chance (SMCs or free municipalities?). But I can fully agree with Tolbert and Zucker when they say:

When some organizational elements become institutionalized, that is, *when they are widely understood to be appropriate and necessary components of efficient, rational organizations* [emphasis added], organizations are under considerable pressure to incorporate these elements into their formal structure in order to maintain their legitimacy. (Tolbert and Zucker 1983, p. 26)

But, as stated, it is quite likely that the early adopters have more problems than the late adopters, and that the early adopters have problems to which a given ideology is particularly relevant. That, related to the motivational anchorage, makes some groups more "ideology-hungry" than others.

The United States in the Twentieth Century

March and Olsen (1983) continued to follow the reforms in the U.S. public sector throughout our century: their interest lay, however, in central government reforms. They noted that major administrative reforms in the United States have occurred frequently but not continuously, just like the reforms in the Swedish public sector. This frequency allows for accumulating experience without producing routines, and therefore is highly interesting for students of organizations. Furthermore, like me, the authors were fascinated with the fact that

. . . those efforts apparently account for an insignificant share of the total administrative changes that occur, are seldom followed by systematic efforts to assess their effects, seem to be a source of frustration and an object of ridicule, became regular and unlamented casualties of experience with trying to achieve significant reform, and yet are persistently resurrected by the political system. (March and Olsen 1983, p. 282)

Analyzing administrative reorganization in the twentieth century, March and Olsen found two main ideologies (or rhetorics). The first was that of orthodox administrative theory, which aimed at efficiency and effectiveness, called for planning and centralization, emphasized economy and control. As March and Olsen demonstrate, this ideology is very persistent and deeply anchored in U.S. culture. Indeed, we recognize in it the rationalization ideology of Tolbert and Zucker study. It is not limited to the U.S. culture: the municipal merger in Sweden was accomplished under this ideology. However, in the latter case the ideology did not play the controlling role: it was a hierarchical and not an ideological reform, as it was ordered from above (Jönsson 1985). In such a situation ideology has a legitimizing, but not a controlling, effect.

The second ideology that March and Olsen observed was what they called "realpolitik" and what I call a "shift in power" ideology. The reorganization, then, is a shift in power, in which the power distribution takes on a different configuration than before. Interest groups, conflicts, power struggles, multiple values, and bargaining are the main concepts. March and Olsen note that the "shift in power" ideology is largely rejected as an official basis for reorganization or, in my terminology, this ideology usually has a status of competitive or subversive ideology.

Another study (DiTomaso 1985) interprets the reorganization of the government under Reagan in terms of the "realpolitik" ideology, whereas the official ideology was "democracy via deregulation." But one can think that, for example, the codetermination reform had the shift in power as its official ideology.

"Democracy via decentralization" is neither of the two, although it has certain formal similarities. Like the rationalization ideology, it assumes a shared goal, but the goal does not consist in the efficient operation of a bureaucratic hierarchy, but in the effective participation in the propagation of a collective good. They are both utopias, and both assume harmony, but their contents differ. Like the "shift in power" ideology, "democracy via decentralization" is a political ideology; different actors and multiple values are recognized, but conflict is not its prominent feature: differences in interests can be negotiated to a consensus. Meyer summarizes it beautifully if somewhat ironically:

The term [decentralization] evokes pastoral democratic imagery about a variety of little organizational units living (presumably peacefully) in some sort of ecological community, each acting autonomously on its own behalf under some sort of general ground rules. (Meyer 1985, p. 6)

When does an ideology acquire a controlling function? What is the relation between the controlling and legitimating functions of ideologies? When is an ideology effective as a control instrument? What are the results of ideological control for organizational members? The next chapter summarizes the findings of the empirical studies, using this list of questions as a structuring device.

6

Ideological Control and the Role of Symbolic Acts in Organizational Life and Studies

IDEOLOGICAL CONTROL IN PRACTICE: A SUMMARY

The studies reported present a picture of ideological control as an organizational process aimed at shaping actions of organizational members by targeting their personal ideologies: the way they see the world in relation to their organization, their vision of the desired state of affairs and of possibilities of moving from a criticized present to a desired future. This target can best be reached by other, organizational ideologies, which are supposed to replace or to reconcile individual ideologies. These organizational ideologies are not ideologies held by organizations. Organizations are heterogeneous social institutions having many members, many groups, and many ideologies. These are ideologies that live in organizations: they belong to people in organizations and relate to aspects of life connected to organizations.

If ideological control is to be effective, the ideology offered by the controller must replace, to a significant degree, other possible ideologies. This is facilitated, as we have seen in the case of the Polish economy, by the anchorage of a new ideology in a broader cultural context that surrounds every attempt at organizing and controlling. The same example demonstrated, however, that such anchorage can be jeopardized by what is seen as insufficient anchorage in reality. Ideologues rarely claim immediate confirmation in observable reality: time delays and practical obstacles are justifications for the gap between ideological vision and present reality. However, when such a gap becomes acutely felt, as in the case of the Polish economy in crisis or the Swedish company on the verge of bancruptcy (Emmaboda Glasverk AB), the ideology becomes ineffective in its influence on organizational action.

Another facet of effective (action-steering) uses of ideology is ideology's responsiveness to needs and wishes felt, independently from ideological persuasion, by the people to whom it is addressed. This requirement of motivational anchorage equals a specific linkage between the targeted ideology (that already held by the members of an organization) and the proposed one. The case of SF AB demonstrated how this motivational anchorage can be seen as ultimately influenced by the cultural context, giving individual motivation of social acceptance.

The cases of the Polish economy and the Swedish companies emphasized intentional, leader-oriented perspective on ideological control. The study of local governments in Sweden highlighted a different perspective on ideological—indeed, all types of organizational—control. Doubtless there are some actors who can be seen as dominant in regard to control attempts. However, a more detailed look at organizational reality, especially one devoid of charismatic leaders, reveals that (at least ideological) control can be used by many different actors, often at cross purposes. Leaders usually try to consciously use ideological control to achieve their goals. Still, leaders are not always clear as to what their goals are, and many other actors try to use the same targets and the same means in attempts at countercontrol. For each ideology there were competing and subversive ideologies, and the attempt to see the whole of the picture led to a more situational concept of control: control as a result of multiple attempts at control by many different actors.

The dissociation of ideological control and charismatic leadership—the possibly impersonal character of ideological control—is a first conclusion that deviates somewhat from similar research reviewed earlier. Another is that in all three cases under study, ideological control was used to accomplish change. Traditionally, as in interest and strain theories of ideological control, it is taken for granted that ideologies serve to maintain the status quo. We can observe now that the two purposes are not mutually exclusive: ideologies can both promote change and/or maintain the status quo. Every successful change agent reaches the point where maintaining the status quo is a positive proof of an accomplished change. Ideologies facilitate social action, whether conservative or revolutionary.

In the next section I shall analyze the mechanisms by which this facilitation is achieved (the organizational functions of ideology). In the sections to follow, I shall move beyond the conclusions emerging from my own and other empirical studies, to speculate about the dynamics that brought ideological control to the fore, and to examine the moral aspects of ideological control. The chapter and book conclude with an attempt to locate ideological control among other organizational phenomena of symbolic character. Throughout the analysis, I shall try to fulfill Geertz's important postulate: that ideologies must not be handled as entities in themselves, but as relationships mediating social and psychological contexts. Ideologies as such have no significance for organizational life: it is the meaning put into them by organizational members that constitutes the link between social and individual, and that decides the function and significance of ideologies (Gertz 1964).

FUNCTIONS OF ORGANIZATIONAL IDEOLOGIES

Ideologies facilitate collective action, and therefore organizational action. This is possible by the separate or joint fulfillment of the functions of motivation, legitimation, and control.

These functions can be fulfilled when an ideology is well anchored in broader contexts: cultural, psychological, and social reality. The most powerful ideologies are those which posesses anchorages in all contexts, but in organizational life we usually have to deal with somewhat defective ideologies. Hence, it is useful to examine the relationships between functions and anchorages in some detail.

The motivating function of an ideology consists in arousing enthusiasm and encouraging social commitment of organizational members. This is likely to happen when the "vision" part of the ideology is perceived as valuable and actions proposed to reach this vision as likely to be successful. This observation gains support in the expectancy theory of motivation (see Atkinson 1958; Vroom 1964; Heneman and Schwab 1973). Thus, a motivational anchorage is the most obvious determinant of the effectiveness of an ideology in its motivating function, as it ties an ideology directly to the desires and needs of people.

However, the cultural anchorage can greatly increase the attractiveness of an ideology (some ideologies are unpopular or boring, even if valuable), and the social reality anchorage permits one to construct expectations concerning the feasibility of proposed actions.

The motivating function of ideology has been discussed, in the context of ideological organizations, as ideological mobilization. Therborn (1980), for example, lists similar anchorages of mobilizing ideologies. "Mobilization by revival" (of past experiences, values, and symbols) is an equivalent of cultural anchorage; "mobilization by example" is reality-anchored. Therborn also introduces what may be called a case of negative motivation: "mobilization by anticipatory fear." The arms race ideology relies heavily on this type of negative motivation.

Brunsson (1985) concentrates on the motivating function of ideologies in organizations, pointing out that the role of organizational ideologies is to create common expectations and thus motivate organizational members. Jönsson and Lundin (1977) and Hedberg and Jönsson (1977) argue in the same vein. All these authors concentrate, much as my own research does, on the role of ideologies as organizational change facilitators.

The legitimating function of an ideology consists in showing, to both internal and external audiences, that what the ideology proposes is considered desirable and acceptable by a given society or community. This is a complex, threefold process.

To be able to fulfill a legitimating function, the ideologies must be legitimate. This condition, true not only for ideologies but for all other symbolic expressions (Thompson 1980; Meyer 1981) has been discussed under the name "symbolic-appropriateness":

. . . even business firms, which are not (supposedly) ideological agencies, nevertheless pay some attention to criteria of symbolic-appropriateness in evaluating and selecting their structures and procedures. They engage in a certain amount of "appearance-management" or "window-dressing." The implication of both terms is machiavellian—that such considerations are really instrumental, aimed at disarming possible critics or opponents, or even attaining more legitimate ends such as efficiency and greater productivity. Certainly these are among the considerations. . . . But a concern for the "appearance" of structures and procedures can also in part from ideological concerns relating to symbolic-appropriateness or inappropriateness. (Thompson 1980, pp. 220-221)

To achieve legitimate status, ideologies must appeal to other symbolic elements that are already considered legitimate. Cultural anchorage is therefore the most relevant in fulfilling this function. But, as what is considered desirable is usually defined in terms of needs, motivational anchorage is also important. And so is reality anchorage: the claim of broken promises very soon becomes a challenge to legitimacy.

Once ideologies acquire legitimate status by relating to other symbolic and nonsymbolic elements considered legitimate, they can serve to legitimize actions of ideology owners and believers in the eyes of internal and external audiences. In that sense, ideologies transcend the present and create the basis for future legitimation. This obvious function of ideologies helps to explain why they are seen solely as devices for maintaining status quo.

And, finally, the least recognized controlling function, the topic of this book. What are the mechanisms that allow an ideology to control the behavior of organizational members? Ideological control, like any other organizational control, is backed by and depends upon sanctions and rewards (Etzioni 1961; Salaman 1980). Yet these sanctions and rewards are different or differently applied than those connected to other modes of control. We must not forget that ideology is the target of ideological control, that is, controllers aim at replacing ideologies already espoused by organizational members. This perspective invites research on attitude change as a help in discussing observations collected in this book.

Attitude change theorists tell us that three attributes of the source of influence determine its effectiveness: attractiveness, power, and credibility (McGuire 1969; Mika 1980). Attractiveness has to do with motivational anchorage, and links the controlling function to the motivational: the most effective control is a self-control. Credibility indicates the role of the cultural anchorage, and links the controlling function to the legitimating: the legitimate status of an ideology supports its controlling power, even if the two can be separate (on illegitimate control means, see Czarniawska 1985b). And, finally, the power of a source pertains to the controlling function as such: are the ideology owners able to provide rewards for adopting an ideology or sanctions for boycotting it?

The sanctions and rewards of ideological control are subtler than other sanctions, or else control changes its character and becomes total (coercion) or ecological (bribes). In none of these cases can one be sure that an adoption of an ideology is an actual attitude change and not just a lip service in order to avoid punishments or to earn rewards. The continuation of the Polish case into the period of martial law and afterward illustrates this. There are severe punishments for some and attractive bribes for others, but there is no illusion about any shared vision or a common ideology.

The genuine rewards or sanctions attached to attitude change are intrinsic or interpersonal. There are several alternative explanations of how the change of attitude occurs (McGuire 1969): learning process (familiarity with new contents, increased knowledge); change of perception (seeing things differently, as a result of persuasion or self-development); striving for consistency (logical or psychological discrepancy between beliefs causes psychic discomfort); functional change (new needs or motives arise, old ones are discarded).

It is easy to see that the four do not exclude each other: learning both helps change perception and produces discrepancies. They can be complementary, or can dominate in different situations. All of them can also be sources of personal and social rewards and sanctions. Learning is a source of self-fulfillment and of group approval, change of perception is very likely a result of group pressure, feelings of inconsistency often arise as a result of confrontation with important others. This complicated process was reconstructed with considerable insight by the converts in the case of Swedish local governments under reform. It should be stressed, and it distinctly emerges from the case studies, that even the most powerful leaders have meager possibilities of intentional and effective control over such rewards and sanctions (which does not prevent them from trying). These are not incentives to be distributed at the end of the month. But that is, actually, a basic hope behind ideological control: that once it reaches its target, it will act invisibly and out of awareness. It holds especially for nonideological organizations, where

. . . the power of ideology operates not only in conjunctures of high drama, but in slow, gradual processes as well. Ideologies not only cement systems of power; they may also cause them to crumble and set them drifting like sandbanks, still there though not in the same place and shape. (Therborn 1980, p. 125)

The line of this discussion may seem to lead to simplistic evolutionary-functionalist arguments: the function of ideologies is to motivate, legitimate, and control, in the service of either change or status quo, and those which can be observed are supposedly those which survived the test of the fittest. Even if I used functionalist literature to explain some of the mechanisms involved, the final interpretation must go further than that. I would like to argue that ideologies' functions are wider and more complicated than organizational, or even societal, interests would define them; that their survival can be supported by both political interests and existential longings; and that, by the same token, ideologies can be opposed, promoted, neglected, and created for a variety of reasons.

Ignatieff (1984), in searching for philosophical grounds of the welfare state, provides us with an existential justification for the existence of ideologies. The thought of Saint Augustine, very indicative for modern Western culture, evokes the distinction between two kinds of freedom: the freedom to make choices and the freedom that comes from knowing that the choice one has made is the correct one:

It has been a recurrent dream of the Western political imagination to fashion a form of society that would so wrap the individual in the fraternity of his fellows that his choices would unerringly reconcile private and public interest, the claims of self and the other, in decisions that the choosing self would know were right. This was the utopia of More, Rousseau and Marx: each understood that freedom and happiness could be reconciled only if individual choice were always anchored in fraternity. But then what is left of freedom if choice is invariably guided by the collective wisdom of the brothers, the citizens, the comrades? (Ignatieff 1984, p. 63)

Is there an escape from being caught between the loneliness of individual choice and the slavery of others' visions? Augustine proposes to look for the second freedom, the certainty of having chosen right, in religion. Are there alternatives? Can we live with uncertainty? Or must we seek comfort in ideologies? According to many philosophers, among them Hume, it is possible to achieve a stoical attitude and carry the burden of loneliness. That sounds like a heroic choice, and it certainly is. On the other hand, people not only suffer from uncertainty and try to avoid it, they also enjoy it and actively look for it: while seeking adventure, while changing their lives, while traveling to unkown places. Maybe ideologies are not needed as much as organizational and political leaders would like us to believe.

I do not have a definite answer to this complicated question. The existential context of organizational ideologies does not easily appear in a formal frame of empirical studies, as the functional does. But these considerations relate back to the interest and strain theories of ideology discussed earlier, although in a new, dynamic perspective (ideologies serve change as well as the status quo). The functionalist perspective accentuates the interest aspect of ideologies' organizational use, whereas the existential perspective focuses on strains that are inseparably a part of human existence, no matter under which political and economic system. Ideologies can be actively used to protect or to promote interests, and they may be created to help to support or to abolish the strain of existence that resides deeper than the theory of class societies would see it. For multiple reasons, then, organizations are full of ideologies. We should study more carefully to what use they are put, when and how, and what consequences they have for us organization members.

IDEOLOGICAL CONTROL AS A DOMINANT MODE OF ORGANIZATIONAL CONTROL

In what circumstances does ideological control become a dominant control mode in an organization? The concept of control cycle responses to decline provides one possible answer (Czarniawska and Hedberg 1985). According to this model, the leadership in organizations responds to crises by a tightening of internal control. The looseness or tightness of control is seen as a distance from the subject of control, or as the degree of discretion and personal control left to the subject. Taking the target of control as a basis for classification of control modes, one can say that the more the target of control becomes the entire person, the tighter control is. Hence, total control is the tightest, and ecological control the loosest, mode of control. When crisis hits, the leadership moves from whichever mode of control was dominant to the next tighter one. If crisis hits a totally controlled organization, the organization will die or will have to be reconstructed on a completely different basis (for example, it can be saved from bankruptcy by a merger that puts in new resources and allows for ecological control).

All cases described show such tightening of control: the leaders of the Polish economy adopted ''propaganda of success'' after a short but intensive period of ecological control, when allocating abundant resources was the main control mode. The crisis of 1973-74 ended ecological control. Similar events took place in the Swedish company, where for several years input (ecological) control of production was predominant, the leadership being busy securing an incessant flow of resources and dreaming dreams of expansion. When awakening came, the new leadership went through the whole cycle, cut off part of the company, and acquired new resources—not enough, though, to permit ecological control as the dominant mode. Thus the next stage, ideological control, became the last. And finally, although not so visibly, the end of ecological control as a dominant control mode in the Swedish public sector slowly brought increased emphasis on ideological control.

One might venture that at least the most prosperous Western organizations, in the late 1960s and early 1970s, reached a level of efficiency that permitted them to make ecological control the dominant mode. The crisis of the second half of the 1970s initiated the control response cycle. Leadership in organizations shifted to a tighter mode: ideological control.

But surely control cycle response is not the only model to explain changes in organizational control modes. A competing explanation may emphasize increasing affluence in Western democracies and neglect short business cycles and involved crises. One can then speculate about the possibility of ideological control becoming the dominant control mode after a long period of action control: direct, technological, bureacratic. Class struggle would go underground, pushed by the technological imperative and the welfare state. Western democracies would become more peaceful and content, or more resigned. Total control is hard to imagine. Increased average education makes people challenge action control. The technological imperative notwithstanding, every operator has an opportunity to learn that machines are not divine, as every clerk notices that rules are breakable without any dramatic consequences. Well-educated members of welfare states do not want to be told what to do. They would much rather do what they think is right.

Hence, whoever wants to control their doing must control their thinking. These control attempts do not have to be intentional to the same extent as with total and action control. Our thinking is controlled by people who do not know about our existence, and could not care less. Mass media and information networks are becoming the main channels of control, even as it is increasingly uncertain who stands at both ends of the information channels.

We are not affluent enough for ecological control, so ideological control is the mode of control that most suits the times.

Still another explanation sees our times as plagued by general social fragmentation, loss of cultural patterns, and anomic social life (Alvesson 1986), resulting in a loss of personal identity and meaning. It can be a matter of discussion whether the desperate search for meaning on a mass scale is a newly acquired luxury of the welfare state's ever-increasing middle classes or the ultimate cry of the oppressed victims of capitalism; but regardless of possible causative explanations, the observation seems plausible. Again, the attempts of the leaders to provide the meaning can be seen as a supply response to a demand or as a manipulation of real needs.

This book does not offer historical material sufficient to turn speculations into empirical theses. Nor is this necessary. As long as all factors operate in the same direction—the increasing dominance of ideological control—the hierarchy of the factors is not that important. The question is, rather: What does it mean for people in organizations?

IDEOLOGICAL CONTROL, LEADERSHIP, AND MEMBERSHIP IN ORGANIZATIONS

The variety of the cases presented demonstrates that no organization can claim a nonideological character: all organizations use ideologies to control. One can discuss how new the phenomenon is, but there is no doubt about its existence. It is equally clear that, at least in the cases under discussion, ideologies come originally from the top of an organization (even if they favor democracy) and are therefore closely related to leadership. These observations fit conveniently into a current consulting trend that advises more leadership and more use of cultural elements (to which ideologies doubtless belong) in performing management functions.

Whereas the previous analysis concentrated on describing and explaining the functioning of ideologies as targets and means of control, we shall now try to address some normative questions that arise. Is more leadership really needed? Is it impossible that an ideology comes from the bottom of an organization? Tentative answers are not, however, in any sense proved by the preceding analysis. Like any other person in pursuit of knowledge, a researcher gains information and understanding of the phenomena under study, which allows for the formulation of judgments predictions, and postulates. But these are by no means proved by the research results. Social scientists cannot, and must not, claim objectivity, predictability, and reliability they cannot deliver. This is, in my experience, important in any communication with managers, who, more often than not, in an interaction with social scientists undergo a dramatic change of attitude toward the latter, who are seen first as magicians and then as charlatans. Shedding the magician's robe should facilitate a sober exchange that could benefit both parties.

Let me review the conclusions of the analysis in light of an ideological assumption—that the greatest possible defect of an organization is the oppression of its members. No matter what other tasks and purposes an organization can have, it ought to create an environment in which human beings can live and work with dignity and which creates an opportunity for development.

As long as it is not used in a manipulative way, ideological control can make a positive contribution to the humanization of the work place. People can try to realize their dreams instead of adhering to the rules, and can see their work as a mission and not as a burden.

Ideologies need not be seen as means of oppression of the powerless. As Clegg and Dunkerley note, ''Dominant ideologies are typically directed at the dominant rather than the subordinate class'' (1980, p. 536). Wosinska (1978) showed empirically that managers were most susceptible to propaganda attempts. Our cases confirm this observation. It was managers and academics who responded to Gierek's appeal for help and cooperation in the first place, with workers somewhat skeptically watching the course of events. It was the managers who were reformed at Svenskt Företag AB. It was the officers who were influenced by the local governments' reform, even if it was supposedly a transitory stage before the reform reached the street level.

Ideological control becomes threatening, however, when it does not tolerate any but the leading ideology. As Milan Kundera put it in his *Unbearable Lightness of Being,* "The criminal regimes were made not by criminals but by enthusiasts convinced they had discovered the only road to paradise." The missionaries turn into inquisitors, and spreading the gospel gives way to a purge. Heretics are persecuted, and skeptics know better than to reveal their doubts. That is especially likely to happen when the ideology ceases to be effective, as in the Polish case. Even if the use of a fire-and-water trial of faith is unlikely in modern corporations, there are more subtle ways of performing similar operations. The attack on ideological pluralism can adopt various convert forms. As Grzyb (1985) notes, managers at present are encouraged to "create organizational cultures" as if they were to operate in a void. No mention of a previously existing, often very strong workers' culture is ever made. Loose coupling, so ardently advised in all other areas of organizational life (Weick 1979), is not recommended for elements of corporate culture, which is to be cohesive.

If ideological control is by definition looser than action control, it does not automatically mean that the employees' area of discretion increases. The leaders, enchanted with the new vistas for control, spend their weekends plotting new ideologies as they used to design strategic decisions. An urge to control (Mandell 1985) results in a flood of visions, "floras of experiments," ideologies concerning total lives of employees and, if possible, their families. The borderline cases of ideological/total control are not so rare in nonideological organizations.

All that stems from the implicit assumption that only leaders (with formal authority) are able to produce (or import) ideologies. The possibility of a variety of ideologies, each produced by an interested group (or by a person who might become a leader or a project manager), does not seem to attract much attention.

The fact that ideological control tends to replace other kinds of control does not prove that control is diminishing. As stated before, there is both more control and more autonomy in today's organizations, and ideological control is a good illustration of that. The kind of control is changing, and compels us—the students of organizations—to pay more attention to phenomena that were receiving but fleeting attention. And these phenomena cannot be safely limited to organizations.

Out of 16 waking hours, at least 8 are spent in organizations. The main source of power experienced by most people in ordinary situations resides there. Be that as it may, the result is that even during those remaining hours we think, fear, and reexperience the previous and the next organizational eight hours. Organizations are, for most people, the main source of their identity. There are very few people in modern Western societies who do not share this fate: some who were not given the chance to join in, like the unemployed; some privileged dropouts, who can afford to stray outside, and some well-meaning alternative seekers who usually end up creating alternative organizations, often taking more than eight hours of peoples' daily life.

It is not fruitful, therefore, to speak about "organizational life" and "private life," "system" and "Lebenswelt" as separate entities. Our life takes place in organizations, and our existential problems are solved or become more complicated inside or outside organizations; organizations are used as a reference to define what is in and what is out. We are organizations; organizations are us. Some would like to claim that they put on organizational costumes at the beginning of the day and shed them at the end. But, in the words of Kurt Vonnegut, Jr., (in *Mother Night*); "We are what we pretend to be, so we must be careful about what we pretend to be."

SYMBOLIC ACTS AND ORGANIZATIONS

The grand, conspicuous symbols are potent only because thousands of subtle, unrecognized symbols embedded in everyday political language and gestures do the real work of evoking beliefs and perceptions. . . . The important and the difficult task for political analysis is to identify the consequences of subtle symbolism, for it is the foundation of political power and of political illusions. (Edelman 1977, pp. 154-155)

This powerful message is addressed to the students of ideological—political—organizations, but if we accept the fact that there are no nonideological organizations, it applies equally to those who study business companies and public administration. In fact, one could say that political symbols lose their importance in everyday life, whereas organizational symbols increase theirs.

In answer to this phenomenon, one might argue, the whole trend of "organizational culture" research has been created. Symbolic organizational acts are given full attention. However, the present state of affairs leaves much to be desired. One serious problem is a joyful confusion of concepts we discussed in Chapter 3. Another peculiarity, chastized by Meyer (1981) and Alvesson (1985a), is that most studies concentrate on trivial or at least "around-the-work-activities," such as coffee breaks or Christmas parties, leaving the actual work content untouched. This has to do with the use of anthropological methods, practiced in primitive societies. While the Christmas party can be seen as an equivalent of a tribal dance, and therefore a legitimate element of "culture," comparing the board of directors with the council of elders seems too daring, and therefore not an appropriate phenomenon for an ethnographic study. Yet many years before the "culture fad" started, this course of action was recommended by far-thinking researchers (Dahl 1961; Olsen 1970; Turner 1971).

Where is the concrete, if so much is symbolic? Surely organizations produce something, pay people, go bankrupt? They do, but proportions between the two spheres vary: some organizations are more oriented toward the concrete; some, toward the symbolic. And if there is no organization in which acts do not have concrete effects (be it wastepaper or energy consumption), there is certainly none free from symbolic acts. Unfortunately, for students of organizations, the concrete and the symbolic are not spheres at all; they cannot be separated and conveniently contrasted like an object and its mirror image (see Harré 1982 on practical and expressive orders). Ideologies can always be traced to material grounds, Therborn (1980) reminds us. The concrete and the symbolic live together like body and soul, but analytical separations tend to concentrate on the body, awarding the soul much less attention. But, as every practitioner knows, this separation is a confidence trick that cannot be maintained for long. Sooner or later we shall have to start to study both of them, and together.

Is the main task of research, as Edelman (1977) postulates, to protect people from exploitation by illusion? To a large degree, yes. But myths, ideologies, and rituals must not be judged exclusively as lies, distortions, and superstitions. They constitute an extremely important emotional and aesthetic aspect of our organizational lives, and as such are indispensable. They can be beautiful or ugly, aggressive or liberating, but they are part of our historical and cultural past, and of our dreams of the future. A disconnected present may not give much room for thought or action.

This does not mean that they should rule our lives. Irrational must make room for rational, emotions for intellect, ideals for reality. Both aspects must cohabit our awareness, and woe to us if one wins. It is as with children's fairy tales: childhood would be sad and dreary without wolves, princesses, and magi, but when a child wakes up every night frightened by a visit from a wizard, we become concerned. A healthy, emotionally balanced child believes in all the fairy tales and yet disbelieves them. This gift should stay with us forever: by thorough rationalization of our adult lives we make them dull and unworthy living. By believing in man-invented monsters, we collapse into fear and the slavery of anxiety.

This appeal for balance may seem unattractive. After all, social scientists, and among them organization theorists, belong with the brothers Grimm. Our task is to produce still new monsters or angels, to prophesy redemption or announce condemnation, no matter whether it is the fairy of rationality or the magus of fantasy whom we are serving. Undoubtedly this is one of our most important roles, but so is its counterpart: sobering feverish sleepers by showing how myths, rituals, beliefs, and ideologies emerge, what influence they have on everyday organizational life, and to what uses and misuses they can be put by willing actors.

Bibliography

Abravanel, H., Mediatory myths in the service of organizational ideology. In Pondy, L. R., Frost, P. J., Morgan, G., and Dandridge, T. C. (eds.), *Organizational symbolism*. Greenwich, CT: JAI, *1982*.

Alvesson, M. *On studying cultural phenomena in organizations: Taking material aspects & the central practices into account.* Working Paper 85-012. Montreal: Concordia University, April *1985a*.

————. On focus on cultural studies of organizations. *Scandinavian Journal of Management Studies*, 1985b, *2(2)*: 105-120.

————. *Organizations, image and substance: Some aspects of the cultural context of cultural management research.* Linköping: University of Linköping: *1986*.

Amnå, E., Brytting T., Ekman, A., Kolam, K., and Montin, S. Kommunal decentralisering. Stockholm: Liber, *1985*.

Atkinson, J. W. Towards an experimental analysis of human motivation in terms of motives, expectancies and incentives. In Atkinson, J. W. (ed.), *Motives in fantasy, action and society*. Princeton: Van Nostrand, *1958*.

Barthes, R. *A lover's discourse*. New York: Hill & Wang, *1981*.

Bednarczuk, L. Nowomowa. Zarys problematyki i perspektywy. In *Nowomowa. Materialy z sesji naukowej poswieconej problemom wspolczesnego jezyka polskiego odbytej na Uniwersytecie Jagiellonskim w dniach 16 i 17 stycznia 1981*. London: Polonia, *1985*.

Beksiak, J. *Zmiany w gospodarce.* Warsaw: PWN, *1982.*

————. The economic crisis in Poland. *Acta Slavica Japonica* 1983, 1:117-125.

Beksiak, J., Buczowski, L., Czarniawska, B., Rebacz, H., and Wawrzyniak, B. *Zarzadzanie przedsiebiorstwami—uczestnikami rynku dobr konsumpcyjnych.* Warsaw: PWN, *1978.*

Bell, D. *The end of ideology.* Glencoe, IL: The Free Press, *1960.*

Bendix, R. The impact of ideas on organizational structure. In Grusky, O., and Miller, G. A. (eds.), *The sociology of organizations: Basic studies.* New York: Free Press of Glencoe, *1970.*

Benson, J. K. Innovation and crisis in organizational analysis. *The Sociological Quarterly,* 1977, *18* (Winter):3-16.

Berg, P. O. *Emotional structures in organizations.* Lund: Studentlitteratur, *1979.*

————. Techno-culture: The symbolic framing of technology in a Volvo plant. *Scandinavian Journal of Management Studies,* 1985. *1*(4):237-256.

Bialecki, I. Solidarity—the roots of the movement. *Sisyphus,* 1982, 3:116-125.

Blau, P. Decentralization in bureaucracies. In Zald, M. N. (ed.), *Power in organizations.* Nashville, TN: Vanderbilt University Press, *1970.*

Bozyk, P. *Marzenia i rzeczywistosc czyli anatomia polskiego kryzysu.* Warsaw: PIW, *1983.*

Brunsson, N. *The irrational organization.* London: Wiley, *1985.*

Burawoy, M. *Manufacturing consent.* Chicago: University of Chicago Press, *1979.*

Burawoy, M., and Lukacs, J. Mythologies of work: A comparison of firms in state socialism and advanced capitalism. *American Sociological Review,* 1985, *50* (December):723-737.

Cartwright, D. Influence, leadership, control. In March, J. G. (ed.), *Handbook of organizations.* Chicago: Rand McNally, *1965.*

Chandler, A. D., Jr. *The visible hand: The managerial revolution in American business.* Cambridge, MA: Harvard University Press, *1977.*

Clarke, J., Critcher, C., and Johnson, R. (eds.). *Working class culture.* London: St. Martin's Press, *1979.*

Clegg, S. *The theory of power and organization.* Boston: Routledge & Kegan Paul, *1979.*

Clegg, S. and Dunkerley, D. *Organizations, class and control.* London: Routledge & Kegan Paul, *1980.*

Cohen, A. *The politics of elite culture.* Berkeley: University of California Press, *1981.*

Cohen, M. D., March, J. G., and Olsen, J. P. A garbage can model of organizational choice. *Administrative Science Quarterly,* 1972, *March*:1-25.

Cohen, P. S. "Theories of myth." *Man,* 1969, *4*:337-353.

Czarniawska, B. *Motywacyjne problemy zarzadzania.* Warsaw: PWN, *1980.*

———. Uczenie manipulowania i manipulowanie uczeniem sie (na przyklad-zie treningu kierowniczego). Paper presented at the session "Manipulacja i obrona przed manipulacja," organized by NSZZ "Solidarnosc," at the University of Warsaw, April 1981.

———. *Controlling top management in large organisations: Poland and U.S.A.* Aldershot, England: Gower, *1985*a.

———. Oscillating between autonomy and control: The Polish economy 1946-1981. *Economic and Industrial Democracy,* 1985b, *6*:325-347.

———. *Public sector executives: Managers or leaders?* Stockholm: EFI, *1985*c.

———. The management of meaning in the Polish crisis. *Journal of Management Studies,* 1986, *23*(3):313-331.

Czarniawska, B., and Hedberg, B. Control cycle responses to decline. *Scandinavian Journal of Management Studies,* 1985, *2*(1):19-40.

Czarniawska-Joerges, B. Decentralization and leadership under stagnation. Unpublished manuscript. 1986. (Available from the author, Stockholm School of Economics, Box 6501, S-113 86 Stockholm, Sweden).

———. Control processes in declining organizations: The Polish economy 1971-1981. *Organization Studies,* 1987, *8*(2):149-168.

Dahl, R. A. The concept of power. *Behavioral Science,* 1957, *2*:201-218.

———. *Who governs? Democracy and power in American city.* New Haven: Yale University Press, *1961.*

Daudi, P. *Makt, diskurs och handling.* Lund: Student-litteratur, *1984.*

Daun, Å. Swedishness as an obstacle in cross-cultural interactions. *Ethnologia Europea,* 1984, *14*(2):95-111.

Dente, B., and Regonini, G. Urban policy and political legitimation: The case of Italian neighborhood councils. *International Political Science Review,* 1980, *2*:187-202.

DiTomaso, N. The managed state: Governmental reorganization in the first year of the Regan administration. In Braungard, R. G. (ed.), *Research in political sociology.* Greenwhich, CT: JAI Press, *1985.*

Donnelly, J. R., Jr., Gibson, J. L., and Ivancevich, J. M. *Fundaments of management: Function, behavior, models.* Dallas: Business Publications, *1978.*

Ds KN 1979: 10. *Lokala organ i kommunerna—modeller för försöksverksamhet.* Stockholm: Liber, *1979.*

Dunbar, R. L. Designs for organizational control. In Nystrom, P. C., and Starbuck, W. H. (eds.), *Handbook of organizational design,* vol. 2, *Remodelling organizations and their environments.* New York: Oxford University Press, *1981.*

Eco, U. *The role of the reader: Explorations in the semiotics of texts.* London: Hutchinson, *1979.*

Edelman, M. *Political language.* New York: Academic Press, *1977.*

Edwards, E. *The contested terrain*. New York: Basic Books, *1979*.

Etzioni, A. *The analysis of complex organizations*. New York: Free Press of Glencoe, *1961*.

―――. Organizational control structure. In March, J. G. (ed.), *Handbook of organizations*. Chicago: Rand McNally, *1965*.

Figa, J. Societal sources of Polish renewal. *Economic and Industrial Democracy*, 1982, *3*(2):117-157.

Forss, K. *Att arbeta utomlands—en bok om kulturskilnader*. Lund: Studentlitteratur, *1987*.

Frankl, V. E. *Man's search for meaning*. New York: Simon & Schuster, *1973*.

Geertz, C. Ideology as a cultural system. In Apter, D. (ed.), *Ideology and discontent*. New York: Free Press of Glencoe, *1964*.

Ge folk ökat infytande. *Dagens Nyheter*, August 2, 1985.

Giddens, A. Agency, institution and time-space analysis. In Knorr-Cetina, K. and Cicourel, A. V. (eds.), *Advances in social theory and methodology*. Boston: Routledge & Kegan Paul, *1981*.

Giddens, A. *New rules of sociological method*. London: Hutchinson, *1984*.

Glaser, B. G., and Strauss, A. L. *The discovery of grounded theory*. Chicago: Aldine, *1974*.

Glowinski, M. Czy nowa polszczyzna? *Polityka*, June 21, 1980, 25(1216):XXIV.

―――. Opis papieskiej podrozy. Z problemow manipulacji jezykowej. Paper presented at the session "Manipulacja i obrona przed manipulacja" organized by NSZZ "Solidarnosc," at the University of Warsaw, April 1981.

Goffman, E. *Asylums*. Garden City, NY: Doubleday-Anchor, *1961*.

Gouldner, A. W. *The dialectic of ideology and technology*. London: Macmillian, *1976*.

Granick, D. *Enterprise guidance in Eastern Europe: A comparison of four socialist economies*. Princeton: Princeton University Press, *1975*.

Grzyb, G. J. Corporate culture and culture in the corporation. Paper presented at the Conference on Critical Perspectives in Organizational Analysis, Baruch College-CUNY, New York, September 1985.

Gustafsson, C. *Om utsagor om makt*. Åbo: Research Institute of the Åbo Akademi Foundation, *1979*.

―――. *Hero-myths and manager-descriptions*. Företagsekonomiska Institutionen Åbo Akademi Preliminära Forskningsrapporter, 2. Åbo Akademi: Department of Business Administration, *1984*.

Harré, R. *Social being*. Oxford: Basil Blackwell, *1979*.

―――. Philosophical aspects of the macro-micro problem. In Knorr-Cetina, K., and Cicourel, A. V. (eds.), *Advances in social theory and methodology. Toward an integration of micro- and macro-sociologies*. Boston: Routledge & Kegan Paul, *1981*.

————. Theoretical preliminaries to the study of action. In von Cranach, M. and Harré, R. (eds.), *The analysis of action: Recent theoretical and empirical advances.* Cambridge: Cambridge University Press. *1982.*

Harré, R. and Secord, P. F. *The explanation of social behavior.* Oxford: Basil Blackwell, *1976.*

Hawkes, T. *Metaphor.* London: Methuen, *1972.*

Hedberg, B., and Jönsson, S. Strategy formulation as a continuous process. *International Studies of Management and Organization,* 1977, 7(2):88-109.

Hedberg, B., Nystrom, P. C., and Starbuck, W. H. Camping on seesaws: Prescriptions for a self-designing organization. *Administrative Science Quarterly,* 1976, *21*(March):41-65.

Hendricks, J. Personal communication, June 1984.

Heneman, H. H., and Schwab, D. P. Evaluation of research on expectancy theory predictions of employee performance. In Scott, W. E., and Cummings, L. L. (eds.), *Readings in human behavior and human performance.* Homewood, IL: Irwin, *1973.*

Heydebrand, W. V. What is a critical theory of organizations? Paper presented at the Conference on Critical Perspectives in Organizational Analysis, Baruch College-CUNY, New York, September 1985.

Hicks, H. G., and Gullett, C. R. *Organizations: Theory and behavior.* New York: McGraw-Hill, *1975.*

Himmelstrand, U. *Social pressures, attitudes and democratic processes.* Stockholm: Alqvist & Wiksell, *1960.*

Ignatieff, M. *The needs of strangers.* London: Chatto & Windus. The Hogarth Press, *1984.*

Jacobsson, B., and Sahlin-Andersson, K. Signalling continuity and reorientation: Balancing between memories and dreams in public organizations. Paper presented at the EGOS Seventh Colloquium; "Challenges to Organizational Authority," Saltsjöbaden, Sweden, June 1985.

Jermier, J. M. "When the sleeper wakes": A short story illustrating themes in radical organization theory. Paper presented at the Conference on Critical Perspectives in Organizational Analysis, Baruch College-CUNY, New York, September 1985.

Jönsson, S. *A city administration facing stagnation.* Stockholm: Swedish Council for Building Research, *1982.*

————. Market or hierarchy? Decentralization in local government. Paper presented at the seminar "Organization and Economy of Local Governments in Change," Vattnahalsen, Norway, August 1985.

Jönsson, S., and Lundin, R. Myths and wishful thinking as management tools. In Nystrom, P. C., and Starbuck, W. H. (eds.) *Prescriptive models of organizations.* Amsterdam: North-Holland, *1977.*

Katz, D., and Kahn, R. L. *The social psychology of organizations.* New York: Wiley, *1978.*

Kets de Vries, M. F. R., and Miller, D. *The neurotic organization*. San Francisco: Jossey-Bass, *1984*.

Kipnis, D. Does power corrupt? *Journal of Personality and Social Psychology, 1972, 24*(1):33-41.

Köhler, W. *Dynamics in psychology*. New York: Liveright, *1940*.

Kuczynski, W. *Po wielkim skoku*. Warsaw: PWE, *1981*.

Kunda G. Organizational ideology as a system of meaning. Paper presented at the First International Conference on Organizational Symbolism and Corporate Culture, Lund, Sweden, June 1984.

————. *Engineering culture: Culture and control in a high-tech organization*. Cambridge, MA: Massachusetts Institute of Technology, *1986*.

Kurczewski, J. The old system and the revolution. *Sisyphus,* 1982, 3:21-32.

Lewin, K. Group decision and social change. In Proshanski, H. and Seidenberg, B. (eds.), *Basic studies in social psychology*. New York: Holt, Rinehart & Winston, *1966*.

Lorsch, J. W., and Allen, S. A. *Managing diversity and interdependence*. Cambridge, MA: Harvard University Press, *1973*.

Lukes, S. *Power: A radical view*. London: Macmillan, *1974*.

Lynn, R., and Hampson, S. L. National differences in extraversion and neuroticism. *British Journal of Social and Clinical Psychology,* 1975, *14*:223-240.

Mandell, A. An urge to control: Reflections on Moses and the rock. Paper presented at the Conference on Critical Perspectives in Organizational Analysis, Baruch College-CUNY, New York, September 1985.

Mannheim, K. *Ideology and utopia*. New York: Harvest, *1936*.

Manning, P. K. Metaphors of the field: Varieties of organizational discourse. *Administrative Science Quarterly,* 1979, *24:*660-671.

March, J. G., and Olsen, J. P. Organizing political life. *American Political Science Review,* 1983, *77*(2):281-297.

Marczak, T. Poczucie rzeczywistosci jako opium. *Aneks,* 1979, *21*:107-114.

Martin, J., Feldman, M. S., Hatch, M. J., and Sitkin, S. B. The uniqueness paradox in organizational stories. *Administrative Science Quarterly,* 1983, *28*(3):438-453.

McGuire, W. J. The nature of attitudes and attitude change. In Lindzey, G., and Aronson, E. (eds.), *The handbook of social psychology,* 2nd ed., Vol. 3. Reading, MA: Addison-Wesley, *1969*.

Meyer, J. W. The also serve: Organizations as ideological systems. Paper prepared for the Conference on Administrative Leadership: New Perspectives on Theory and Practice, College of Education, University of Illinois at Urbana-Champaign, July 1981.

————. Decentralization and legitimacy in public administration. Paper presented at the seminar "Organization and Economy of Local Governments in Change," Vattnahalsen, Norway, August 1985.

Mika, S. Some determinants of source credibility. *Polish Psychological Bulletin,* 1981, *12*(2):79-86.

Minc, B. The reasons for the Polish crisis of 1980-1981. *Economic and Industrial Democracy,* 1982, *3*(2):141-158.

Mintzberg, H. *The structuring of organizations.* Englewood Cliffs, NJ: Prentice-Hall, *1979.*

Morgan, G. Paradigms, metaphors and puzzle solving in organization theory. *Administrative Science Quarterly,* 1980, *25*(4):605-622.

―――. More on metaphor: Why we cannot control tropes in administrative science. *Administrative Science Quarterly,* 1983, *28:*601-607.

Nord, W. R. Dreams of humanization and the realities of power. *The Academy of Management Review,* 1978, *3*(3):674-679.

Ohlsson, B. H. *On the politics of reorganizing.* Gothenburg: BAS, *1978.*

Olsen, J. P. Local budgeting: Decision making or a ritual act? *Scandinavian Political Studies,* 1970, *5:*85-118.

O'Toole, J. J. Corporate managerial culture. In Cooper, C. L. (ed.), *Behavioral problems in organizations.* Englewood Cliffs, NJ: Prentice-Hall, *1979.*

Percy, W. The symbolic structure of interpersonal process. *Psychiatry,* 1961, *24:*39-52.

Perrow, C. *Complex organizations: A critical essay.* New York: Random House, *1976.*

Peters, T. J., and Waterman, R. H., Jr. *In search of excellence.* New York: Harper & Row, *1982.*

Pfeffer, J. The ambiguity of leadership. *The Academy of Management Review,* 1977, *2:*104-112.

Pfeffer, J., and Salancik, G. R. *The external control of organizations.* New York: Harper & Row, *1978.*

Pinder, C. C., and Bourgeois, V. W. Controlling tropes in administrative science. *Administrative Science Quarterly,* 1982, *27:*641-652.

Pohorille, M. Questions of income distribution in Poland. *Economic and Industrial Democracy,* 1982, *3*(2):159-176.

Rosen, M. The reproduction of hegemony: An analysis of bureaucratic control. In *Research in Political Economy,* Vol. 8. Greenwich, CT: JAI Press, *1985.*

Sabini, J., and Silver, M. *Moralities of everyday life.* New York: Oxford University Press, *1982.*

Salaman, G. *Work organizations.* London: Longman, *1979.*

―――. Organizations as constructors of social reality (II). In Salaman, G., and Thompson, K. (eds.), *Control and ideology in organizations*. Milton Keynes; England: The Open University Press, *1980*.

Schein, E. H. *Coercive persuasion*. New York: Norton, *1961*.

————. The role of the founder in creating organizational cultures. *Organizational Dynamics*, 1983, *12*(1):13-28.

Scott, R. W. *Organizations: Rational, natural and open systems*. Englewood Cliffs, NJ: Prentice-Hall, *1981*.

————. Centralization and decentralization in interorganizational systems. Paper presented at the seminar "Organization and Economy of Local Governments in Change," Vattnahalsen, Norway, August 1985.

Selznick, P. *TVA and the grass roots: A study in the sociology of formal organizations*. New York: Harper & Row, *1966*.

Silverman, D. *The theory of organizations*. New York: Basic Books, *1971*.

Sjöstrand, S.-E. *Samhällsorganisation*. Lund: Doxa, *1985*.

————. The dual function of organizations. *Erhvers ökonomisk tidsskrift*, 1986, *50*(2):96-116.

Skinner, B. F. *Walden Two*. New York: Macmillan, 1948, *1970*.

Skenbar frihet—mer byråkrati. *Dagens Nyheter*, April 22, 1985.

Smircich, L., and Morgan, G. Leadership: The management of meaning. *Journal of Applied Behavioral Science*, 1982, *18*(3):257-273.

Stites, R. Festival and revolution: The role of public spectacle in Russia 1917-1918. Paper presented at the conference "Symbols and Rituals. The Esthetics of Political Legitimation in the Soviet Union and Eastern Europe," Uppsala, October 1985.

Tannenbaum, A. S. Control in organizations: Individual adjustment and organizational performance. *Administrative Science Quarterly*, 1962, 7:236-257.

Therborn, G. *The ideology of power and the power of ideology*. London: Verso, *1980*.

Thompson, J. D. *Organizations in actions*. New York: McGraw-Hill, *1967*.

Thompson, K. Organizations as constructors of social reality (I). In Salaman, G., and Thompson, K. (eds.), *Control and ideology in organizations*. Milton Keynes, England: The Open University Press, *1980*.

Tolbert, P. S., and Zucker, L. G. Institutional sources of change in the formal structure of organizations: The diffusion of civil service reform, 1880-1935. *Administrative Science Quarterly*, 1983, *28*:22-39.

Turner, B. A. *Exploring the industrial subculture*. London: Macmillan, *1971*.

Van Maanen, J. Working the street; A developmental view of police behavior. In Jacob, H. (ed.), *The potential for reform of criminal justice*. Beverly Hills, CA: Sage, *1974*.

Van Maanen, J. and Barley, S. R. Occupational communities: Culture and control in organizations. In Staw, B. M., and Cummings, L. L. (eds.),

Research in organizational behavior, Vol. 6. Greenwich, CT: JAI Press, *1984.*

Vroom, V. B. *Work and motivation.* New York: Wiley, *1964.*

Weber, M. *The theory of social and economic organization.* New York: Free Press, *1964.*

Weick, K. E. *The social psychology of organizing.* Reading, MA: Addison-Wesley, *1979.*

————. Sources of order in underorganized systems: Themes in recent organization theory. In Lincoln, Y. S. (ed.), *Organizational theory and inquiry.* Beverly Hills, CA: Sage, *1985.*

Whitley, R. Organizational control and the problem of order. *Social Science Information,* 1977, *16*(2):169-189.

Whyte, W. H. *The organization man.* New York: Simon & Schuster, *1956.*

Williamson, O. E. The modern corporation: Origins, evolution, attributes. *Journal of Economic Literature,* 1981, *19*(December):1537-1568.

Wosinska, W. *Psychologiczne wyznaczniki efektywnych oddzialywan propagandowych w zakladzie pracy.* Katowice: Uniwersytet Slaski, *1978.*

Zimbardo, P. G., Haney, C., Banks, W. C., and Jaffe, D. Psychology of imprisonment. In Rubin, Z. (ed.), *Doing unto others.* Englewood Cliffs, N.J.: Prentice-Hall, *1974.*

Index

About The Author

Barbara Czarniawska-Joerges is associate professor of business administration at the Economic Research Institute, Stockholm School of Economics.

Until 1981 she was assistant professor at the Faculty of Psychology, University of Warsaw. She spent the academic year 1981/82 at the Sloan School of Management, M.I.T., in Cambridge, Massachusetts. Subsequent appointments were at the Science Center Berlin, and the Swedish Center for Working Life.

Dr. Czarniawska-Joerges has published widely in the area of business administration in Polish, her native language. Her first book in English was entitled *Controlling Top Management in Large Organisations* (1985). Her articles have appeared in *Scandinavian Journal of Management Studies, Economic and Industrial Democracy, Journal of Management Studies,* and *Organization Studies.*

Dr. Czarniawska-Joerges holds an M.A. in social psychology from the University of Warsaw and a Ph.D. in economic sciences from the Central School of Planning and Statistics, Warsaw.